THE MAKING OF SILICON VALLEY

A ONE HUNDRED YEAR RENAISSANCE

Ward Winslow, Editor

Published by the Santa Clara Valley Historical Association
1995

525 Alma Street
Palo Alto, California 94301, USA
Telephone:(415) 323-0765
(800) 425-3463
Facsimile : (415) 323-0766
Internet: SCVHA@Batnet.com

Book, video and CD-ROM purchases
(800) 425-3463

Publisher: John R. McLaughlin
Editor: Ward Winslow
Project Manager: Gina Woolf
Art Director: Keith Costas
Photo Editor: Clarissa Turner
Corporate histories: John K. Waters, Ward Winslow
Transcriptions: Susan Bright Winn
Copy Editor: Theresa Navarro

First Edition

Library of Congress Catalog Card Number: 95-72050
Winslow, Wardell V., 1927-

The Making of Silicon Valley: A One Hundred Year Renaissance
Ward Winslow, editor
152 pages
9 x 12 inch format
Includes bibliography and index
ISBN 0-9649217-0-7

Published in Palo Alto, California, USA
Printed in Singapore

The Santa Clara Valley Historical Association
gratefully acknowledges the support of the following corporations
as Premier Sponsors in the preparation of this book;
the videotaping of interviews with more than 60 company founders, scientists, inventors,
entrepreneurs, scholars, and others immersed in the phenomenon that is Silicon Valley; and
the production of the related videotape, narrated by Walter Cronkite:

Applied Materials, Inc.

Cirrus Logic Inc.

Hewlett-Packard Company

International Business Machines Corporation

Network General Corporation

Oracle Corporation

Other Sponsors are denoted by the corporate histories
that are included in this book
in an order corresponding to the date of their founding
or of their first presence in Silicon Valley.

In addition to their support for the production
of this book and the related videotape,
the sponsoring corporations and firms,
in keeping with the educational and cultural purposes
of the Santa Clara Valley Historical Association,
are distributing copies of the book and videotape
to high schools, colleges, and universities of their choice.

Table of Contents

PREFACE

The constellation known today as Silicon Valley represents the choicest achievements of America's high technology during the 20th century—a century during which the United States surged to world technological leadership and poured out inventions, innovations, and developments in a volume unprecedented in history, either in quantity or quality.

The purpose of this book is to collect and pass on to new generations an understanding of how this phenomenon came to be. Thus, the Santa Clara Valley Historical Association has sought to explain the events and conditions that prepared the locality for its present role, to set down the broad outlines of what happened both before and after 1970, when Silicon Valley got its nickname, and to list what appear today to be the key inventions. In this book, the text of the chronological chapters is interlaced with the histories of companies that started operations here in the same eras. Read together, these chronicles will, we hope, give the reader a general picture of the making of Silicon Valley.

In saying so, we must add that the picture does not include every detail we or others might wish. It is not exhaustive, not complete. Indeed, a history that purports to cover a subject as broad and diverse as this one almost up to its date of publication cannot be complete. Even if it could, the notorious difficulty of assessing the historic import of recent events would render interpretation chancy, at best.

So not every event is reported, not every company is mentioned, not every issue is explored in depth. Other authors have illuminated certain facets brilliantly; their works will be found listed in a bibliography. Neither do we claim to be teachers explaining each wondrous product or principle.

In conducting scores of interviews with company founders, inventors, engineers, entrepreneurs, venture capitalists, scientists, professors, and others with an insider's understanding of a technology, a company, or the Valley itself, our questions have tended to follow a consistent pattern. We have asked what motivated these individuals, when their interest in science or technology began, how they went about forming their companies, what attitude they took toward the risk of failure inherent in creating a start-up, which hurdles were the most challenging to leap, and how their enterprises grew. We have sought to bring out why they deemed Silicon Valley the right place for their firms, and what they would advise young persons considering careers as entrepreneurs or creators in high technology.

Most of these interviews were videotaped. Thus, they establish a database of a sort—one in keeping with public suggestions about recording the Valley's history made in print by James J. Mitchell, business editor of the *San Jose Mercury News*, and Michael S. Malone, the foremost author on the subject of Silicon Valley. This database is providing much of the material for a videotape intended to accompany this book , and may later be available in more depth on CD-ROM or future forms of electronic storage. It constitutes an exceptional (and almost impossible to duplicate) record of the founders and pioneers telling their stories, animated by their distinctive facial expressions and tone of voice. The book does not begin to encompass the entire content of these interviews, or the personalities of their subjects, but we hope it does derive some flavor from them, for they are a remarkable group of human beings.

The publisher and editor and their associates are particularly grateful to six Premier Sponsors of this project—Hewlett-Packard Company, International Business Machines Corporation, Network General Corporation, Oracle Corporation, Applied Materials, Inc., and Cirrus Logic Inc. Their interest transcended the notion of simply having their own stories told; beyond that, they wished to have the broader history of this regional miracle recorded.

We are indebted to the other sponsors as well. Some of them have exerted extraordinary effort to fit their own histories into the general context of the times of their birth pangs and struggles to succeed. Our request was that they allow their histories to be related in terms easily understood by a high school sophomore. In these accounts, the reader will find jewels of information and understanding both large and small.

The Palo Alto Historical Association has served as a cosponsor of the Santa Clara Valley Historical Association in this project, lending its name, the run of photographic files, and the prospect of serving as a repository for the film collection. Steven Staiger, PAHA's historian and a City of Palo Alto reference librarian, has been of great assistance. Gail Woolley, a past PAHA president and former mayor of Palo Alto, was instrumental in shaping our endeavor, as were PAHA presidents Crystal D. Gamage and Judy Leahy. Susan Bright Winn, a PAHA officer, worked with exceptional devotion on transcribing interview tapes.

We are indebted also to Donald Koijane, president of the Perham Foundation, Inc., for access to its photographic collection and for his counsel, particularly regarding aspects of radio. The Perham Foundation Electronics Museum is endeavoring to move to a building at the San Jose Historical Museum.

At Stanford University, Dean of Engineering James Gibbons has been of great assistance. So have Margaret Kimball and Linda Long at the Special Collections Department of Green Library, and Henry Lowood, the bibliographer for history of science and technology collections at the Stanford University Libraries. We are grateful for the help of the Stanford Office of News and Publications.

At the California History Center at De Anza College, Lisa Christiansen, librarian of the Louis Stocklmeir Regional History Library, assisted with both file research and photos.

At the *San Jose Mercury News*, Executive Editor Jerry Ceppos, Managing Editor David Yarnold, Candace Turtle, and Library Director Gary Lance arranged for us to use many historic photographs.

Santa Clara Valley Historical Association board members James Harrison, Jim Hudspeth, Sheri Midgely, and Sally McLaughlin helped shape the project. Others who labored to bring it to life included Gina Woolf, Gail Murphy, John Napier, Charlotte Weber, Ken Allison, Sven Jensen, Josh Wagner, Paul Salcedo, Paul Marca, and Glen Park.

For legal counsel we are grateful to Tom Alderman, John Arnold, Rich Gray, and Mark Waite. Those who acted as sounding boards and advisers include Kevin Burr, Grace Ensign, Robert McLaughlin, Jill Vandervort, Bill Brauner, Rob Walker, and Holly Winslow.

Walter Cronkite was not only thoroughly professional but also gracious in working with us, as was his assistant, Marlene Adler. Dennis McNalley of The Grateful Dead arranged the use of musical excerpts as well as an interview with the late Jerry Garcia.

Many corporate personnel went out of their way to facilitate our work. In particular, we wish to thank Karen Lewis, the archivist of Hewlett-Packard Company, for her advice and suggestions, and Rachel Stewart and Penny Geiber at Intel Corporation for their help.

Although these and many other individuals have lent a hand in advancing this project, the accuracy of this book is strictly the responsibility of the editor and our staff. We sincerely hope it will be useful in educating the world—and especially students—about the making of Silicon Valley.

Ward Winslow
Palo Alto, California
September 30, 1995

INTRODUCTION

The Making of Silicon Valley began on the simple premise that the technology of Silicon Valley has impacted the world more than any other occurrence since the Renaissance. From this idea the project moved forward. We tried to imagine ourselves in 500 years and asked, "Who would future scholars and history buffs want to interview on video tape from 20th century Silicon Valley?" That was our guiding principle however politically incorrect. Each of the sixty-four individuals we interviewed was incredibly brilliant and inspirational. Many of their quotes are printed throughout this book. It is our intention to have each video interview available through local libraries and to make pictures and text accessible through the Internet or on an interactive CD-ROM.

As the producer, I usually wrote a letter or presented a short synopsis to each interviewee as to why the Historical Association was comparing Silicon Valley to the European Renaissance (1350 to 1600 A.D.). Here are a few of the parallels.

The European Renaissance began at the onset of the Black Death and perhaps because of it. The preplague economy was predicated on cheap, abundant human labor. Most of the real property belonged to the nobility and the clergy, and the common people were unlikely to move up from their lower caste. Reading and writing (in Latin) were primarily the preserve of the church and nobility. Then came the Black Death.

The Black Death was almost beyond comprehension. It swept through villages and the countryside without resistance or prejudice as to its victims. The nobility, the clergy, the rich, the poor, the doctors... many died horrible deaths within a few days. Religious and medieval medical solutions (often intertwined) were ineffective. In three years almost one half of the human population perished. Feudal Europe was never again the same. The Black Death, or plague, made its initial impact in 1347 A.D. and continued to depopulate Europe for the next 100 years.

A curious consequence of the Black Death was that many who survived the plague became affluent through inheritance or because the value of human labor increased. There was, quite literally, almost twice the number of houses, property and farm animals per person as there had been before the onset of the plague. The survivors of the Black Death were empowered with a new wealth and a radically different view of the world. After all, they had survived, but they knew that death could be just around the corner.

The conditions were ripe for change and innovation. Cheap labor was being replaced by relatively sophisticated labor-saving technology. The new rich demanded the best. The entrepreneurs of the Renaissance period pushed early technology to the limit to make the best hats, gowns, shoes, and cutlery. The perfection of eyeglasses, gunpowder, clocks, water pumps, fishing, mining, the printing press, and publishing were just a few of the technological improvements. Serfdom, people indentured to the land or nobility, eroded as the value of labor increased.

What survives the Renaissance is the astonishing art of Leonardo da Vinci, Michelangelo, Raphael, Titian, Van Eyck, Dürer, and Holbein; and the fabled voyages of discovery by Christopher Columbus, Amerigo Vespucci, Ferdinand Magellan, and Vasco da Gama. Their lives and forms of non-traditional expression were a means of trying to impact humanity positively. They succeeded.

Preplague historical records as well as written communications were primarily the preserve of the church and nobility. Johannes Gutenberg's invention of movable type sought to solve the problem of printing wills, an important industry after each plague. He's more famous for printing giant-sized Bibles for the church. It was nearly forty years later near Venice, Italy, when Aldus Manutius took the new technology of Gutenberg to transform civilization at all levels with the publishing of portable books. The effect was immediate and profound.

Within a century, much of the European world became literate. Printers were publishing books in over 80 European cities. The church and nobility no longer had a monopoly on written or printed information. What was more important, it became possible for a printed idea to be spread throughout Europe within months. This new freedom of information, the great flow of ideas, created a period that demonstrated technological application and improvement. A synergy. An Italian's method of architecture could be copied and improved upon by a Spaniard, and again by the Germans. No longer was a long journey to a foreign land necessary to "memorize" a technique. The new method could now be printed in the universal language of Latin. The famous 19th century Swiss historian, Jacob Burckhardt, wrote that the Renaissance is "a civilization which [was] the mother of our own."

The devastation of the Black Death is inevitably compared to 20th century's flu epidemic and World Wars I and II. The fear and desperation brought about by these events must be understood in the same context as that of the Black Death. The sense of urgency was similar. For example, the development of modern radar by the Varian brothers, allowing a plane to "see through the clouds," was executed with great urgency to stop Hitler's genocidal onslaughts.

"As a pilot [Sig Varian] said to himself, what could happen in Europe and Asia in bombing cities could happen here too. If Hitler wanted to, he could organize a secret air force base in South or Central America, attack American cities and go away undetected."

— Edward Ginzton, cofounder, Varian Associates.

After World War II, a different kind of urgency filled the air: the real possibility of nuclear holocaust. The Cold War lasted from the 1950s through the 1980s with the threat of nuclear annihilation hanging over mankind (especially over Silicon Valley).

Many people believed that a nuclear war would take place — the only question left unanswered was: When would the nuclear holocaust begin? This created an urgency to live one's life as if there were no tomorrow. The desire to follow one's dreams was, in many cases, stronger than the urge to follow traditional pathways.

"After a party there was an automobile accident and Paul was killed, there were four of us in the car, we were all injured but Paul died, so in the aftermath of that, that whole little scene kind of pulled together and kind of gained a kind of sense of purpose. So that was kind of like one of those little kicks in the ass that you need to get you going, that was one of my kicks. It worked pretty well."
— Jerry Garcia, founder, Grateful Dead

It's no coincidence that much of the great rock and roll music of the 1960s and 1970s emanated from the sons and daughters of the Silicon Valley work force: The Grateful Dead, Santana, Pablo Cruise, Jefferson Airplane, Quicksilver Messenger Service, Credence Clearwater, Journey, Fleetwood Mac, and more. The affluence of the Valley and a sense of urgency, coupled with youth's rejection of tradition, were primary factors that led to the formation and success of these music groups.

The sense of urgency affected Silicon Valley in a variety of ways. Because of former Governor, Senator and entrepreneur Leland Stanford founding a university based on collaboration and real application of learning, the culture of the Valley was already very supportive of entrepreneurs and risk takers. It already had a history of independence and entrepreneurship. Hewlett's and Packard's partnership in 1938 and the decision of eight young men in 1957 to start their own semiconductor company with little experience or money were seminal points in Silicon Valley's growth

The advent of the personal computer was a reflection of the rebellion against the data collection monopolies of the federal government and giant corporations. The crusade of Jobs and Wozniak at Apple Computer was driven by a goal of giving this vast power of information to the ordinary person.

"Apple was the primordial, prototypical start-up in every respect. And more importantly, it was informed with true evangelism, a true sense of mission.... There was a true sense of changing the world. So, the atmosphere was one of youth. It was one of passion. It was one of creativity. It was one of very little structure, but a process that everybody understood. And you might not codify that process, but you knew it was there. And the process was to get something done and make a difference. And, Steve Jobs kept using the phase, 'Give something back.' And so, there was really a sense of not being part of a company, but being part of a cause or a crusade."
— Fred Hoar, early Apple Computer marketing director, president of Miller Communications

The most important parallels between the European Renaissance and Silicon Valley are quite striking. First is the sense of urgency, primarily because of the ongoing resurgence of the Black Death during the Renaissance period and in modern times, the anticipation of a nuclear holocaust. Second, the zeal for entrepreneurial change and innovation. Within the walls of hundreds of Silicon Valley corporations are dedicated engineers, scientists and entrepreneurs that are driven to cure an illness, develop a faster computer chip or write useful software. Third, the worldwide impact of information. From the monopoly of written communications by the church and nobility in the 14th century and the monopoly of computer information by government and large corporations in the 20th century — to Renaissance publisher Aldus Manutius starting the process of making books for everyone and Apple Computer ushering in the age of the personal computer. And fourth, in Renaissance Italy, the entrepreneurial culture was sponsored by the great patrons of the arts, such as Cosimo de' Medici the elder of Florence, Italy, who funded talented artists, musicians, scholars, and craftsmen. In Silicon Valley, the foundations of this culture of risk and invention are the result of many. If anyone can claim the title of the "father of Silicon Valley," it would be the late Stanford dean of engineering and provost Fred Terman. However, this area's sponsors include the vast resources of the venture capital industry and the thousands of residents who invest in ventures they believe to have merit.

During the European Renaissance, Gutenberg's invention of movable type, the introduction of paper from the East, and Aldus' publication of books created a new world — one that still inspires creative genius to this day. With the worldwide proliferation of the personal computer and the emergence of the Internet, there is no question that the communications explosion has already transformed the world. We may find that the next phase of communication will come in from the air.

"Within 10 years, we'll have portable PCs that will be virtual books, and you'll be able to through the air download a new book or download a magazine or newspaper, and a lot of people will start using that as their primary medium."
— Jim Clark, founder, Silicon Graphics and Netscape

"It is perhaps the most significant renaissance that has ever occurred in the history of science. It has happened very fast simply because the technologies that are being developed here have moved forward with almost breakneck speed, but the profound impact they're having on technology—I can't think of any other comparable change anywhere in the history of the world—and this technology, it's not just a change in technology, it's a change in the way we live, the way we work, the way we think, the way we communicate. So it is not only a technology renaissance, it is a renaissance in the broader sense of the word."
— William J. Perry, founder of ESL and U.S. secretary of Defense

We have been fortunate to have interviewed, on camera and in depth, many of the Valley's most successful scientists and entrepreneurs, all of whom started their careers with little or no money. In 1994, the direct gross revenues that this small group of people created from their ingenuity was more than $60 billion. It is most astonishing that these Silicon Valley revenues are not produced from natural resources such as wheat, marble, or oil; they are primarily generated from inventions, mental prowess, and by people following a different path with the willingness to take a risk.

John R. McLaughlin
Palo Alto, California, USA
November 1, 1995

Silicon Valley Achievements

Silicon Valley's copious outpouring of inventions, scientific discoveries, adaptations, and developments makes a long list. The Valley's contributions to civilization include, in part:

Long distance high-voltage transmission, the amplifying vacuum tube, the first commercial radio broadcast, long distance continuous-wave radio transmissions, mobile radio systems development, the klystron tube and microwave radar, electronic measuring devices, nuclear induction applications, the X-ray microscope, traveling-wave tube development, silicon crystal-growing, programmable hand-held calculators, videotape and VCRs, development of the junction transistor, linear accelerators for particle physics research and cancer treatment.

Swept-back aircraft wings, nuclear magnetic resonance, random access computer storage; disk drives, integrated circuits, planar processes, lasers, semiconductor large-scale integrated memory, silicon gate arrays, microprocessors, light-emitting diodes (LEDs), personal computers, open-heart surgery, ink-jet printing, high resolution aerial photography, spacecraft heat shields, batch processing of micromachined devices, gene-cloning and gene-splicing.

Video games, silicon compilers, automated semiconductor manufacturing equipment, field programmable gate arrays, prodigious advances in artificial limbs and sensory aids, robotics, genetic engineering, satellite technology, 3-D computing, and a host of other wonders.

Stanford University Nobel laureates with King Carl XVI of Sweden in 1984 (from left: Henry Taube, Arthur Schawlow, Robert Hofstadter, Paul J. Flory, Paul Berg, King Carl Gustaf, Burton Richter, William Shockley, Kenneth Arrow, Linus Pauling, and Arthur Kornberg).

Chapter 1: The Making of Silicon Valley — An Overview

Strong waves of creative energy have flowed in recent decades from a place known as "Silicon Valley," encircling — and changing — the world. How it happened is the subject of this book.

The phenomenon known since the 1970s as Silicon Valley can be traced to origins in the 1890s when Leland Stanford established a university at Palo Alto and urged that its students not only gain knowledge but be able to apply their learning in the real world. Pioneer professors, especially in the sciences and engineering, took Senator Stanford's cue and collaborated with nearby industries from the outset.

As the 20th century began, wireless radio captured public attention, soon after introduction of the telegraph and the telephone. The wonder of Morse Code or the human voice riding mysterious air waves excited adults and youths alike. Palo Alto became an early test bed for radio experiment. Later it became the locale for development of continuous-wave transmission powered by arc generators, thanks to engineer-entrepreneur Cyril Elwell. Elwell employed a radio research team including Lee de Forest, who in 1906 had invented a three-element vacuum tube in New York. In 1912 the team discovered that the tube, which de Forest called the audion, could be rigged as an amplifier. This was a major breakthrough. It was first exploited in long-distance telephony, then in radio, and later in other tube-powered devices, such as radar, television, and computer systems, over a span of about 40 years.

Radio took root on the San Francisco Peninsula. In San Jose, Charles Herrold began the first regularly scheduled radio broadcasts in 1912. In Palo Alto, the Federal Telegraph Company established by Elwell created ocean-spanning networks, supplying U.S. Navy communications during World War I. Many of Stanford University's electrical engineering graduates worked at Federal for a time. Tube-making companies were founded on the Peninsula, and a technical community built up. At Stanford, Frederick Terman became the leading academic authority on radio engineering.

California goldminers — 1849

At Stanford, physics professor William Hansen developed insights that were applied by the Varian brothers in the klystron tube and later in linear accelerators, which proved useful in smashing atoms and treating cancer. A generation of microwave engineers emerged, helping to win World War II and afterward exploiting television and long-range communications.

In the postwar years, Hewlett-Packard Company became the dominant local electronics company, developing measuring equipment, scientific instruments, a programmable calculator, and ultimately computers, printers and other peripherals. HP also served as a management school. Droves of its graduates became mainstays of other companies.

Meanwhile, in 1947 a Bell Labs team led by William Shockley invented the transistor, which after years of development would replace the electron tube. Shockley returned to Palo Alto, his boyhood home, to commercialize the transistor. Eight crack young scientists and engineers he had recruited as assistants broke away and formed Fairchild Semiconductor. Led by Robert Noyce, they invented a practicable integrated circuit and delved into the chemical magic of planar processes. Solid state physics took hold, ultimately chasing away most

1769 Spaniards camp near S.F. Bay.

1776 Pueblo of San Jose founded.

1849 Gold Rush populates California.

1850 U.S. admits California as 31st state.

1864 Peninsula railroad is completed.

1876 Bell invents the telephone.

1888 Heinrich Hertz demonstrates radio waves.

1891 Stanford University classes open.

1901 Marconi sends trans-Atlantic radio signal.

1906
Earthquake, fire devastate San Francisco.

1912
Audion tubes amplify fly's footsteps.

1917
Palo Alto firm supplies WWI Navy radios.

1927
Fred Terman begins to teach at Stanford.

1937
Varian brothers build klystron at Stanford.

1939
Bill Hewlett & Dave Packard start company.

1941
Wounded U.S. enters WWII.

1946
SRI founded to do research for the West.

San Francisco Peninsula

Peninsula microwave development. From crude ICs that many companies built on their own for a time, the art developed more and more specialties.

IBM's invention of the random-access memory system in San Jose energized the infant computer industry and grew an entire new branch, disk drives.

The Cold War and the space race gave big boosts to electronics and aerospace companies. Semiconductor development surged. Then Fairchild Semiconductor all but self-destructed. That explosion left dozens, nay scores, of glowing embers in the Valley.

Intel was one of the companies formed by Fairchild refugees. Intel pioneered the art of putting read-only computer memory on chips, and then scored the most important breakthrough of the latter 20th century, the creation of the microprocessor. Ted Hoff proposed the architecture and Federico Faggin made it work. These computers on a chip, growing ever more powerful, at length enabled Silicon Valley's microcomputer industry to dethrone the Boston area minicomputer companies. The advent of the personal computer, pioneered by young Steve Wozniak and Steve Jobs, also was a vital element in the computer revolution.

The phenomenal development of semiconductors and electronics fed upon itself. Ambitious engineers, entrepreneurs, and managers began to see Silicon Valley as a mecca. They came sometimes directly to industry, sometimes with a stop at Stanford or the University of California at Berkeley for a Ph.D. or an MBA — to learn and to look for a new wave to ride.

Opportunity could be read in the many personal and corporate successes. The local climate was benign, the culture open and exciting. The Valley was experiencing a wave of intellectual and creative energy at least the equal of any in the European Renaissance four to five centuries earlier. Investors were attracted, and a venture capital community evolved.

Semiconductor manufacturers at first made their own processing equipment, but as processes became more complex, equipment manufacturers took over that job, became a separate industry, and eventually automated their clever systems.

Research may be more advanced in Silicon Valley than anywhere else, and not only in the universities and SRI International (a precedent-setting applied research facility), not only in the government's Ames Research Center and Lawrence Livermore Laboratories, not only in such world-renowned industrial research centers as IBM's and HP's and Lockheed Missiles & Space Company's and the Xerox Palo Alto Research Center, but in almost every high technology company. As for development, industries have honed their timetables, telescoping the time required to bring a product to market — a better quality product than the one it replaced.

Management processes created in the Valley are likewise noteworthy. Hundreds of new techniques and styles have blossomed, and some of them are exemplary. Law practice relating to high technology has been drastically altered. Marketing communications specialists have broken new ground. Desktop publishing arose in the Valley, as did the quantum jump in movie special effects powered by 3-D computing.

Sandhill Road 1904

Stanford's first graduation

Another industry, biotechnology, sprang from discoveries of gene-splicing and gene-cloning at the great Bay Area universities.

Part of what makes Silicon Valley tick is the sharing of knowledge. Boundaries that once isolated companies or academic departments are breached not only in industry but on campus, creating cross-fertilization and new synergy. For example, visionaries have applied fast computers to new kinds of drug research, and advances in lasers to new medical devices. Many a technical or management bottleneck was broken by sharing information and experiences, usually not directly with a competitor but with a peer or a mentor.

Primary dissemination of knowledge occurs at the universities and at exceptional four-year colleges and two-year community colleges. San Jose State University is renowned for supplying high technology companies with more engineers than come from all other colleges combined.

Even companies accustomed to doing everything "in house" learned that that was no longer necessary. The Valley had grown an infrastructure. This supporting network of suppliers and service providers allows companies to focus on their special skills and hire help to fill the gaps. They get quick service on components, design, and other orders.

Riches have rewarded the Valley's output. To some participants, money is a great motivator; others thrive on the sheer excitement of helping to create something new and different. Even after 25 or 30 years of start-up companies granting stock options, initial public offerings still create instant multimillionaires at high tech companies. Beyond the lifestyles it enables, money is an essential fuel for such companies, for the costs of building plants and ramping new production have soared while the interval between new products has shortened.

"Silicon Valley" is a term coined by a trade press editor in 1971. Insiders who use the term mean more than a place, they mean a culture too. The heartland runs from San Carlos and Redwood City through Menlo Park, Palo Alto, Mountain View, Sunnyvale, Cupertino, Santa Clara, San Jose, and Milpitas. Strong outposts are in Fremont, Hayward, San Leandro, Emeryville, Berkeley, San Ramon, Pleasanton, San Rafael, South San Francisco, Scotts Valley, and Monterey. Given today's digitized home offices and telecommuting (or the local tradition of starting a business in one's garage), power centers might also be found in such lush foothills residential towns as Hillsborough, Woodside, Portola Valley, Atherton, the Los Altos area, Saratoga, Monte Sereno, and Los Gatos.

Not every Silicon Valley leader views its burgeoning as a renaissance. However, most do, and at present they can see no end to it. Technologies will inevitably change, but they expect the entrepreneurial and creative drive to carry far into the 21st century, and perhaps much farther.

Experimental pointing device on computer screen 1964

1952
IBM sets up laboratory in San Jose.

1953
Varian firm first to settle in industrial park.

1956
Lockheed moves division to Sunnyvale.

1957
Soviet Union orbits Sputnik.

1958
NASA created; Stanford prof proposes laser.

1959
Noyce-led 8 build integrated circuit.

1966
Particle physics research starts at SLAC.

1969
U.S. astronauts first to land on the Moon.

1890
The Battle of Wounded Knee is last major clash of U.S. troops and Indians.

New York conducts first execution by electrocution.

Sherman Antitrust Act begins federal effort to curb monopolies.

1891
Forest Reserve Act empowers president to establish national parks.

London is world capital of finance, shipping and insurance.

1892
Ellis Island opens as immigration depot in New York.

1893
Financial panic begins 4-year depression.

1894
First showing of Edison's kinetoscope (motion pictures).

1895
Marconi experiments in wireless telegraphy.

Röntgen first to demonstrate the X-ray.

Stanford University (circa 1898)

Chapter 2: Leland Stanford Founds a University Dedicated to Making Its Graduates Useful to the World

Two centuries ago, the Santa Clara Valley and the San Francisco Bay lay almost untouched by human endeavor. The thin population of Costaño Indians, inhabitants for many thousand years, had walked softly on the land, leaving little but shell mounds as traces of their hunter-gatherer culture. The oak-studded valley floor, with willow thickets near the shore and dense chaparral edging the foothills and the timbered mountains, showed only the creations of nature.

European explorers came starting in 1769—Spanish soldiers and Franciscan padres. Slowly they built presidios (army bases) and a chain of missions. The missions became hubs for agriculture and for attempts to convert and domesticate the indigenous "heathens" to Christianity. Farming proved to be the more successful activity.

Late in 1777, California's first civil settlement was established in the heart of the Santa Clara Valley—*el Pueblo de San José de Guadalupé.* Frequent flooding led to the town's relocation away from the river in 1797; even then the initial count of 66 settlers had not doubled. Early in the 1820s, Mexico broke away from Spain and began to rule in Alta California. The jurisdiction of the San Jose *ayuntamiento* or town council spread northward into what would later become San Mateo and Alameda counties. After control of the missions passed from church to civil authorities in the mid-1830s, some of Mission Santa Clara's grazing lands in the present Mountain View-Palo Alto area were granted to individual owners.

In the 1839-1844 period, San Jose wrested from San Francisco the honor of being *la cabrera del partido,* or capital of the district. But that was not to last, for San Francisco was ideally suited for water transportation in the prime of the sailing ship, and about 1845 its population began to swell. Just before the Gold Rush, the town founded in 1835 had grown to 200 shacks and adobes inhabited by about 800 whites.

In 1846, American Capt. John B. Montgomery sailed the sloop of war Portsmouth into the bay, landed with sailors and marines and raised the U.S. flag in the plaza. The 1849 Gold Rush gradually filled San Francisco harbor with deserted ships, their crews having rushed to the diggings. But it was not the miners who got rich—those who fed, provisioned, and otherwise catered to them did.

Rapid growth helped win California statehood in 1850, and San Jose enjoyed a brief time as the first state capital. But valley and Peninsula land remained in farming and ranching, and thus stayed open, generally in large tracts. Logging stripped the mountains to the west to supply San Francisco's ravenous appetite for building materials.

In 1863, an upstate New York-born lawyer who had prospered as a merchant supplying miners was elected governor. Leland Stanford served for only two years, but long afterward was esteemed as the "Civil War governor" who had exerted his powers to keep the state in the Union and aid President Lincoln. He and three compatriots, Charles Crocker, Mark Hopkins, and Colis P. Huntington, had already organized the Central Pacific Railroad; later they completed the western part of the first transcontinental railroad, and Stanford himself drove the golden spike. They also bought out the San Francisco and San Jose Railroad, which had reached Mayfield (now Palo Alto's California Avenue district) in 1863 and San Jose early the next year.

In 1874, Stanford, who presided over the Central Pacific (later the Southern Pacific), moved from Sacramento to a Nob Hill mansion in San Francisco. A fancier of trotters and racehorses, he sought a country retreat. He found one near *el Palo Alto,* the landmark redwood where the first exploring Spaniards had camped in 1769. There the governor built up a horse farm that became America's most famous. Gradually he acquired more than 8,000 acres.

Stanford and his wife, Jane Lathrop Stanford, were touring Europe when their only son, Leland Jr., 15, contracted typhoid fever and died in Italy in 1884. The heartbroken parents soon decided that his memorial would be a university, with their Palo Alto estate part of its unprecedented $20 million endowment. Plans for the project dominated Stanford's attention, even after the California Legislature elected him a United States senator. In business he had met many eastern college graduates whose education had left them ill-prepared for the workaday world. One of the standards he set was that the university qualify its students for "personal success and direct usefulness in life." David Starr Jordan, chosen as the founding president, fully respected this wish as well as Stanford's insistence that the sciences be given their proper place, not denied it as on most other campuses of that era.

On October 1, 1891, Leland Stanford Junior University opened. Enrollment at the tuition-free institution almost doubled expectations—440, about one-quarter women. By the second semester it had swelled to 559, many more than were then enrolled at the University of California at Berkeley. The professed wish of the grieving Stanfords that "The children of California shall be our children" had begun to be fulfilled. And from its start, the university served not just the children of California but of the world.

Pioneer professors welcomed the practicality Senator Stanford preached and President Jordan championed. Particularly in the sciences and engineering, they set a tradition of intensive field work, as well as classroom lectures, laboratory experiments and book study. Both as consultants and as teachers, they made league with leaders of industry, business, and government in their fields so their students would understand what needed to be done in the "real world."

Herbert C. Hoover arrived in Palo Alto early for tutoring before he joined the pioneer Class of 1895; he can be called the university's first student. His rapid rise to the top ranks of mining engineers offered one example of Stanford's success in educating students for useful lives. About two decades later Hoover organized World War I food relief, then served as a Cabinet officer and President of the United States.

Palo Alto, a town laid out by Timothy Hopkins with the help of a loan cosigned by Leland Stanford, grew quickly, although the land had been left in hayfields until 1890. Its residents voted to incorporate in 1894. From the start, Stanford professors played key roles in the town's civic affairs. Engineering Professors Charles D. (Daddy) Marx and Charles B. Wing were leaders in gaining city ownership of all major utilities—a rarity, and the base for a strong infrastructure when high technology came to town in the 1950s.

Before the turn of the century, electrical engineering Professor Frederic A.C. Perrine teamed up with students to field-test a locally developed high-potential oil switch. It made possible construction of 40,000-volt lines across the state, harnessing water power in a locale far from coal sources. In 1905, Professor Harris J. (Paddy) Ryan, a transmission research pioneer at Cornell University, came west to head the Stanford electrical engineering faculty. He too promoted university-industry cooperation, as did another man who joined the faculty in 1904, William F. Durand, the leading authority on airplane propeller design.

Senator Stanford's death in June 1893 plunged the university into a money crisis, While lawsuits tied up his estate, Mrs. Stanford devoted intense effort, personal income, and even her jewels to seeing that the university survived. The estate won in court. Under the founding grant, Mrs. Stanford controlled the endowment until 1902, when she empowered the Board of Trustees. A new round of campus construction was almost completed when she died in 1905.

At that point, Stanford did not rank among the world's foremost universities. But its foundations were well laid. Its blending of the ideals of excellence, practicality, and success bore a portent of revolutionary advances.

Leland Stanford

Victory in Sino-Japanese War gives Japan power over Korea and Formosa.

1896

Democrats nominate Bryan after "Cross of Gold" speech.

1898

Battleship Maine blows up at Havana.

War ends with Spain ceding Philippines, Puerto Rico, Guam to U.S., making Cuba independent.

U.S. annexes republic of Hawaii.

Marie, Pierre Curie discover radium.

1899

U.S. declares Open Door Policy for China.

1900

In China, U.S. helps suppress "Boxer" rebellion.

Hatchet-bearing agitator Carrie Nation begins raiding saloons.

1901

Texas has first important oil strike.

McKinley dies of anarchist's bullets.

1903
Wilbur and Orville Wright complete first powered flight in an airplane.

1904
"Muckraker" Ida Tarbell publishes her History of Standard Oil.

1905
Defeat by Japan checks Russia's Asian expansionism.

Albert Einstein states his Theory of Relativity.

1906
Earthquake and fire devastate San Francisco; quake damage heavy at San Jose, Stanford.

1907
16 battleships of U.S. "Great White Fleet" cruise around the world.

Steamship Lusitania crosses Atlantic in 5 days.

1908
Henry Ford produces the first Model T automobile; price: $850.

Federal Telegraph

Chapter 3: Wireless Radio Possibilities Fire Experimenters

Communication by wire had come to the Peninsula in 1853, when California State Telegraph lines were strung from San Francisco to San Jose, then east to Stockton, Sacramento and Marysville. Completion of the San Francisco-San Jose rail line a decade later added stations and Morse Code operators at depots.

Alexander Graham Bell's invention of the telephone in 1876 rang a San Jose harmonic in 1880 when the Sunset Telephone Company was organized there. Telephone service grew slowly until almost the turn of the century, then spurted.

Wireless telephony was in the wind as Stanford University opened in 1891. In 1888, Heinrich Hertz had demonstrated that James Clerk Maxwell's predictions concerning electromagnetic waves were correct, at least for short distances. The press reported Hertz's experiments and those of Guglielmo Marconi, an Italian physicist working in England, who in 1898 broadcast a Morse Code signal across the English Channel. Reading of this and witnessing experiments by his Stanford physics professor, a science-minded student from San Jose named Charles David Herrold repeated Marconi's tests in his home laboratory. He managed to send signals over a distance of one mile.

Cyril Elwell

A few years later, the *San Francisco Call* used wireless to flash the news that a troop ship bringing American soldiers home from Manila was near the Golden Gate. Soon military networks were being linked up.

When Marconi sent a dot-dot-dot signal (the Morse letter S) across the Atlantic in 1901, his feat was widely reported. At Stanford, it stirred keen interest among the professors — and their sons. "Wireless" experiments required no complex equipment — a cylindrical Quaker Oats box wound with copper wire, a crystal and a "cat's whisker" wire were about all it took to tune in.

Meanwhile, inventors were aiming to improve Marconi's transmitting system. In San Francisco, Francis McCarty, 17, son of Leland Stanford's head coachman, began to develop a promising damped-wave method. But in the aftermath of the 1906 earthquake, the youth was killed by a runaway horse. Two investors, the Henshaw brothers of Oakland, asked Professor Ryan at Stanford to name someone to continue McCarty's work. Ryan turned to Cyril Elwell, a recent engineering graduate who had succeeded in developing electric smelting techniques.

Elwell set up shop in Palo Alto, where radio had gained a toehold. Douglas Perham had built the first radio spark transmitter in town in 1906, and later moved it to his house and machine shop at 913 Emerson Street. Three amateurs were active locally: James Arthur Miller, who in 1907 had built a 75-foot antenna mast and set up the first radio station in town, and two professor's sons, Daddy Marx's boy Roland and George Branner. Elwell bought a house at 1451 Cowper Street and put up two 75-foot wooden masts. Turning the bungalow into a wireless telephone station, he broadcast a wavering version of "The Blue Danube" to stations about five miles away in Los Altos and Mountain View.

Federal Telegraph's Palo Alto switches

After testing the McCarty system for a year, Elwell concluded that it was inadequate — only continuous waves (C.W.) would serve the need he saw for reliable commercial wireless transmissions that could compete with cable companies for lucrative traffic. Knowing Danish scientist Valdemar Poulsen had produced C.W. with an arc converter, Elwell telegraphed Poulsen asking how much he wanted for U.S. rights. The price proved too steep; the Henshaws withdrew from the project and Elwell bought their equipment for $250. Then he sailed to Denmark and made a deal with Poulsen. Returning with a small arc converter he bought, Elwell failed to elicit backing in New York, where promoters of Marconi's system and others had given wireless a bad reputation. Back in Palo Alto, Stanford President Jordan offered to invest $500, and with that as a cachet, Elwell enrolled other faculty members — particularly Professor Marx — as investors in the Poulsen Wireless Telephone and Telegraph Company, founded in 1909.

Elwell bought Perham's house and shop in 1910. It served as the apparatus factory for what, in 1911, became Federal Telegraph Company. The company demonstrated 50-mile, two-way C.W. communication between Sacramento and Stockton. Next came a 2,100-mile transmission to Honolulu, using 300-foot masts designed by Professor Wing. Then the company built a U.S. network of 16 high-power wireless stations, and in 1912 opened a San Francisco-Hawaii commercial wireless route.

The arcs enabled Federal to focus signals in a narrow band, unlike the older systems, but they needed continuous improvement. Lee de Forest, who in 1906 had invented a three-element vacuum tube he called the audion, asked for a job in 1911 and Elwell made him research director. Technician Charles Logwood and telephone engineer Herbert Van Etten were added to form a radio research team. Besides improving C.W. and the arcs, the trio experimented with de Forest's audions, which had only been applied as a wireless signal detector. Cascading a series of tubes, they developed the first genuine amplifier, showing how it could make a fly's steps on a sheet of paper sound like an army's marching boots, and airing voices 2 1/2 blocks from the lab.

The team also noted "squeals and howls" in a repeater circuit — signs of feedback that could create a self-regenerating oscillation. Decades later the U.S. Supreme Court awarded the feedback invention patent to de Forest, based on the lab notes. The audion, after improvement in the East, became the key component of all radio, telephone, radar, television, and computer systems until the invention of the transistor in 1947.

About the time Elwell was airing "The Blue Danube" in 1909, Charles D. Herrold, by 1909 nicknamed "Doc" because he headed a college in San Jose for training engineers and telegraphers, broadcast voice and music from "San Jose Calling," a station he first identified as FN. Herrold used an arc transmitter of his own design. In 1912 Herrold began regularly scheduled broadcasts — apparently America's first. His station later became KQW and then KCBS. Among his listeners in 1914 was a Stanford faculty member's son, Fred Terman, who with Herbert Hoover Jr., the son of future U.S. President Herbert Hoover, had built a spark set.

Arc converter at Federal Telegraph

1909

Adm. Robert Peary reaches North Pole on 6th try.

French aviator Louis Bierot makes first airplane flight across the English Channel.

Newsreels become part of popular movie fare.

1910

The Union of South Africa is formed.

Boy Scouts of America founded.

1911

Marie Curie wins her 2nd Nobel Prize.

Norwegian explorer Roald Amundsen reaches the South Pole.

First flight across U.S. takes 82 hours.

1912

British ocean liner Titanic sinks off Newfoundland.

American Girl Guides founded; name changed to Girl Scouts a year later.

Ottoman Empire loses almost all lands in Europe.

Stanford Engineering Crest

Chapter 4: An Industry Rises—Federal Telegraph

As 1913 dawned, Federal Telegraph Company was off to a great start. It had the best technology of the day, a capable chief engineer in Cyril Elwell, and an outstanding research team led by Lee de Forest. And it was able to hire the cream of Stanford's electrical engineering graduates. But the company was due to experience problems that became common in Silicon Valley later on—defections, spinoffs and money troubles. Even so, it was upward bound.

De Forest soon left to sell his audion improvements, to which Federal had only "shop rights." They were bought by American Telephone and Telegraph, whose engineers had been unable to develop repeaters to boost long-distance calls beyond 900 miles. Elwell, meanwhile, had lost financial control of the firm to promoters whose manipulations embarrassed him and Professor Wing as directors representing the Stanford investors. He joined a British company in 1913.

Besides the research team disbanding, Federal lost two Danes who had come over to install the Stockton-Sacramento circuit, engineer Peter V. Jensen and mechanic C. Albertus, as well as the first American electrical engineer Elwell had hired, E.S. Pridham, a talented Stanford graduate. The three quit to develop a loudspeaker, and the moving-coil principle they used in work at Napa and Oakland led to formation of a successful company, Magnavox. Such speakers were to be used at public assemblages and in millions of radio receivers.

Federal still had plenty of talent. Leonard Fuller, a Cornell graduate with wide-ranging experience, and Harold Elliott took the lead as Federal began developing U.S. Navy communications. Roland Marx helped perfect the giant arcs. Elliott later developed a radio broadcast receiver for mass production, and many radio pushbutton tuning devices. After the United States entered World War I in 1917, Federal ballooned to 300 employees, housed in a plant on El Camino Real south of University Avenue. Near the end of the war Federal built a giant station near Bordeaux, France, with James Arthur Miller the principal engineer. Its arcs were workhorses at all major American naval bases.

During the war, the government ordered the few widely scattered civilian broadcasters, including Doc Herrold, to shut down. Herrold turned to training military operators.

After Armistice Day in 1918, a new technological era began. Arc transmitters were being outmoded by improved tubes. Herrold, for one, had to junk the broadcast equipment he had invented and replace it at an exacting cost.

Although government work slacked off as peace settled in, radio was due for great expansion. Federal carried on its long lines and shore-to-ship traffic, and also developed new products. Frederick Kolster, who had invented the radio direction-finder in 1913, worked as Federal's chief research engineer from 1921 to 1931. Kolster produced a radio compass and radio receivers and did experiments with big parabolic directional antennas.

Lee de Forest, center, at 1915 exposition

1915
German Zepplin airships bomb Britain in first airship raids; (1915-16).

1917
Homeland promised for Jews in Palestine through the efforts of the Zionist movement and the creation of the Balfour Declaration.

Russian Revolution and the abdication of the tsar. Lenin's bolsheviks take power.

1919
Ernest Rutherford, English scientist, splits the atom.

The Allies and Germany sign the Treaty at Versailles.

1920
Amendment to the U.S. Constitution prohibits the sale of alcohol in the U.S.; (1920-33).

1922
The tomb of Tutankhamen is discovered in Egypt.

Federal Telegraph's station near Bordeaux

In 1921, Federal built a transmitting station in the Palo Alto baylands, employing a 626-foot mast designed with the help of Professor Wing. The Marsh Station was known by the radio call letters KWT (later KFS). Mackay Radio and Telegraph Company, soon to become a unit of International Telephone and Telegraph Company, bought the station in 1927 to use for point-to-point and ship-to-shore communications.

The Marsh Station switched from arcs to more efficient vacuum-tube oscillators in 1935—a conversion marking the start of shortwave radio. The mast stood until 1960.
Federal's transition from arcs to tubes spanned the years 1927 to 1934. A key figure in that era was engineer Charles V. Litton, a Stanford graduate who became fascinated with tube-blowing as a teen-ager.

In 1931 Federal Telegraph's manufacturing operations were moved to New Jersey after company officials decided Palo Alto was too far away from sources of supplies, skilled labor, and key markets. ITT eventually swallowed the company. Among the Federal employees who decided not to go East was Charlie Litton. Instead, he started his own company in Redwood City, where his tube-developing skill was a boon to remaining Peninsula radio operations. Another who stayed behind, Gerhard R. Fisher, developed the M-scope, a detector of metal and water as deep as 20 feet underground.

Frederick Emmons Terman, the son of famed Stanford psychologist Lewis Terman, also worked at Federal Telegraph briefly in the course of taking chemistry and electrical engineering degrees at Stanford. Then Terman went on to the Massachusetts Institute of Technology to earn a Ph.D. under Vannevar Bush. Terman was slated to teach at MIT, but while home at Stanford for the summer came down with tuberculosis. In 1927 Harris J. Ryan offered Terman a half-time position at Stanford teaching radio engineering courses. After fully recovering, Terman stayed at Stanford to run a new lab. Before long he had written the leading textbook on radio engineering, an earlier name for electronics.

Dirigible over Moffett N.A.S.

A few other facts about the 1912-32 era foreshadowed later epochs. Brothers Russell and Sigurd Varian, Palo Altans as boys, had moved to Halcyon, south of San Luis Obispo. To enroll at Stanford to study physics, Russell Varian walked the 200 miles to the campus. Meanwhile, another professor's son who spent his boyhood in Palo Alto from 1913 to 1922 was a science-struck fellow named William Shockley.

The year 1931 brought another development that was destined to take the area into outer space: Bay Area people raised more than $476,000 to purchase and sell for $1 to the U.S. government the land for what became Moffett Field, initially a naval air station for dirigibles.

Despite the Depression and Federal's departure, there was light at the end of the tunnel.

1923
Canadian physician, Dr. F.G. Banting discovers insulin, treatment for diabetes.

1927
The U.S. and England establish commercial radiophonic communication.

Lindbergh completes the first non-stop solo flight from New York to Paris.

1928
The Graf Zepplin, a German airship, makes the first commercial round trip across the Atlantic.

Alexander Fleming of England discovers penicillin, the first antibiotic.

1929
Wall Street Stock Exchange crash leads to the Great Depression in the U.S.; 2300 U.S. banks fail.

1930
Gas turbine is invented.

future Armored Gun System is designed for airdrops; its 105mm cannon is loaded automatically

From a distinctive heritage dating back to the 1880s, a leading defense contractor has emerged. In 1994, FMC Corporation's Defense Systems Group merged with Harsco Corporation's BMY Combat Systems Division to form United Defense, L.P. FMC manages the limited partnership and owns 60% of it; Harsco owns 40%.

The FMC story began in 1883 when retired inventor John Bean moved to a 10-acre almond ranch in Los Gatos, California. A scale infestation was threatening his crop, and he bought a pump to treat the problem. When the pump did not work to his satisfaction, Bean invented a better one. After 20 years of small-scale pump sales, the Bean Spray Pump Company was formed. In 1910, the growing company moved to Julian Street in nearby San Jose.

A year earlier, the Anderson-Barngrover Manufacturing Company, another Santa Clara Valley farm machinery manufacturer, also had relocated to Julian Street. In 1928, Bean Spray Pump purchased Anderson-Barngrover, forming the John Bean Manufacturing Company. A year later, in 1929, the name was changed to Food Machinery Corporation to reflect the company's diverse product lines.

For years, the company continued to grow and diversify, providing farm, fire-fighting, and automotive service equipment, as well as agricultural chemicals. Then came World War II. To keep its nine plants open, FMC began subcontracting work for the war effort. In 1940, company engineers developed the first amphibious landing vehicle, called the "Water Buffalo." FMC built 11,000 of these vehicles during World War II, significantly contributing to the war in the Pacific and the D-Day invasion.

After the war ended in 1945, FMC again diversified and grew, expanding into industrial chemicals, and in the late 1940s, the name changed to Food Machinery and Chemical Corp. The 1950s marked a new era for FMC, with the creation of the Ordnance Division to produce a new steel-hulled, tracked military vehicle, the T18. New production and office facilities were built on Coleman Avenue in San Jose, near FMC's fire-fighting and agricultural equipment plant. Then the corporate offices moved to Coleman Avenue in 1951.

In 1955, after FMC built several thousand T18 and derivative vehicles, the U.S. Army opened competition for the next generation troop carrier, the M113 armored personnel carrier. FMC would ultimately produce more than 80,000 M113-based aluminum-hulled vehicles during 33 years of production, including missile carriers, mortar carriers, command posts, and scout vehicles. Fifty percent of the M113 family of vehicles went to the U.S. Army, and the other half were shipped overseas to support allied militaries.

In 1956, FMC underwent a major leadership change and began an even more prosperous era. New businesses were added each year; 200 new products were introduced; 80 patent applications were filed; and employment rose to 16,000. In 1961, the San Jose-based company received a new name: "FMC Corporation."

Worldwide expansion continued throughout the 1960s, with FMC's entry into cellophane and synthetic product manufacturing. The company produced a mobile floating assault bridge in 1964, salvage equipment for retrieving nuclear bombs from the ocean in

1967, and Dimazine, a liquid rocket propellant used in the 1969-72 moon landings.

The early 1970s brought a national economic slowdown during which the corporate offices were moved from San Jose to Chicago in 1972. But by the end of the decade, corporate sales were up to more than $3 billion. The San Jose-based defense group continued its success with the M113 armored personnel carrier and other military vehicles, such as the LVTP7 armored amphibious landing vehicles for the U.S. Marine Corps.

In 1978, the defense group began work on a program that would boom throughout the 1980s: development and delivery of Infantry Fighting Vehicles (IFV), for which it received an initial $200.8 million government contract. In 1981, the IFV was dubbed the Bradley Fighting Vehicle after five-star U.S. Army Gen. Omar Bradley. At one point, backlogged orders for Bradleys exceeded $1.2 billion.

After initial production was won by FMC in 1980, the company produced 6,724 Bradleys through February 1995. Multiple Bradley-derivative vehicles have been developed by the company: the Multiple Launch Rocket System, the Electronic Fighting Vehicle System, a Command & Control Vehicle, and the Bradley Fire Support Vehicle. United Defense is now in the process of upgrading the Bradley with the latest electronic systems and technology to significantly enhance it for the integrated, digitized battlefields of the 21st century.

The Bradley was extensively deployed during Operation Desert Storm. When the conflict ended, former Secretary of Defense Dick Cheney paid a visit to the San Jose defense group and touted the value of the Bradley. Cheney declared: "There have been no other weapons systems in our history that performed better in war and combat than the Bradley."

Today, United Defense's Ground Systems Division sites in San Jose/Santa Clara, York, Pennsylvania, and Aiken, South Carolina, continue a long tradition of providing the world's best tracked vehicles to the U.S. Armed Forces. Based in Silicon Valley, the Ground Systems Division's Engineering Center of Excellence is developing cutting-edge technology for the next generations of tracked vehicles, including:

- Creating composite material armor plating for the Army's Composite Armored Vehicle Advanced Technology Demonstrator, a lighter, faster, less detectable vehicle.
- Integrating high-tech electronics into existing tracked and wheeled vehicles for the Army's Force XXI Appliqué program, the military's next-century vision for seamless communication, coordination, and technological integration on the battlefield.
- Development of the Armored Gun System, a lightweight, easily deployable, highly maneuverable tracked vehicle.

The 1994 partnership which created United Defense melded DSG's strengths with those of York-based BMY, a fabricator of armored combat earthmovers, recovery vehicles, and howitzers. Today, with 6,000 diverse employees worldwide, United Defense is the premier supplier of tracked, armored combat vehicles to the United States and allied security forces.

United Defense's AGS with Level 3 armor is descended from famed Bradley fighting Vehicle

Stanford University

1933
Adolf Hitler, chancellor and virtual dictator, leads extreme national Nazi party in Germany. Hitler establishes a totalitarian state and uses millions of Jews for slave labor in concentration camps where they suffered starvation, torture, and ultimately death.

1934
Fleeing from the Chinese Nationalist Army, Mao Zedong and Zhu De lead communists on Long March through China hoping to find sanctuary.

1935
W.H. Carothers of the U.S. invents polyamide fibers (including nylon in 1937).

Chapter 5: The Great Depression—Back to the Lab

The Depression held the United States in a paralyzing grip, crimping industrial operations and pinching funding for costly academic research. It was a time to learn, apply brainpower, and make do in the laboratory at minimal cost.

Federal Telegraph's move East had closed the Palo Alto-Stanford area's major production plant, but it left behind some engineers and skilled workers who chose to stay in the West. At the university, Fred Terman was firmly entrenched as the leading U.S. academic man in radio engineering. Even before becoming Electrical Engineering department head in 1937, Terman encouraged his students to start businesses. He took them to San Francisco to visit places like Heintz & Kaufman's radio plant and Philo Farnsworth's television development workshop.

John Kaar began developing mobile radio communication from his Menlo Park garage, later moving Kaar Engineering to Palo Alto. First he equipped the dogcatcher with a moble radio. Then, with Terman's advice, Kaar installed a police-fire network linking Palo Alto and nearby towns. Messages went from base to vehicles in the field at first, but soon became two-way.

Leonard Fuller, Federal's ex-chief, headed electrical engineering at the University of California. He arranged for Federal to give Berkeley a leftover 80-ton, 1000-kilowatt arc generator. With it, atom-smashing pioneer Ernest O. Lawrence built his first successful cyclotron.

Stanford Union

In 1934, Eitel-McCullough began fabricating vacuum tubes in San Carlos, enlarging a Bay Area tube production cluster dating back to 1916-20. Charles V. Litton, another ex-Federal star, set up Litton Electronics in Redwood City to produce custom vacuum tubes and tube-making machinery. Litton patented some multigrid tubes in which oscillations occurred and assigned the patents to Stanford.

At Physics Corner on campus, William W. Hansen, Russell Varian's former roommate, was new on the faculty. Hansen hankered to do nuclear research, but the money shortage kept him from using X-ray tubes and the Ryan High Voltage Laboratory. Using resonance techniques instead, he developed a cavity resonator to accelerate electrons. The copper container could be made to act as an excellent radio-frequency circuit, capable of developing extremely high voltages with modest power input. He called it a *rumbatron*.

Rus Varian, meanwhile, had worked for a time as a chemist assisting Philo Farnsworth, and then in the East. His younger brother, Sigurd, a former Pan American World Airways pilot in Latin America, persuaded Rus to come home to Halcyon and set up a lab. Sig envisioned an aircraft navigation and detection system to save pilots' lives in darkness or storms. Hearing

...after crash

Daredevil Sig Varian's Plane...

about Hansen's rumbatron, Rus Varian wrote him to say it might fit their needs. So a collaboration began that brought the Varians to Stanford. They got physics lab space plus $100 a year for materials in exchange for half of any eventual patent earnings.

In their collaboration, Rus Varian generated ideas, Bill Hansen sifted out the promising ones, and Sig Varian built prototypes. By mid-1937, Russell had proposed a way to make the rumbatron an oscillator or amplifier that modulated streams of electrons into powerful waves. Sigurd sought such pulses of high-frequency energy to bounce off aircraft, ships, or ground features—the principle of radar. Soon they had a new electron tube. They named it the klystron.

The invention excited the Sperry Gyroscope Company of New York. Sperry licensed the klystron patents and, for an extra $1,000, the patent rights Charles Litton had given Stanford. Litton insisted that the money go to the engineering school for research on electronic tubes. Fred Terman allocated it to graduate student support, specifically for David Packard, one of "Terman's boys" who had been working on vacuum tubes at General Electric in Schenectady, N.Y.

Packard and a radio lab buddy, William R. Hewlett, had talked about starting a company after graduating in 1934, but GE's offer of a job took Packard East. Hewlett, as a Stanford graduate student, applied a Terman suggestion in building a continuously variable broadcast tuning condenser. After a year at MIT, Hewlett returned to Palo Alto and joined Packard in perfecting the audio oscillator. It became the basis for the partnership they established formally on January 1, 1939. Initially, their "plant" was the one-car garage of a house David and Lucile Packard rented at 376 Addison Avenue in Palo Alto.

Terman, who invested cash of his own in the start-up, once told how he could tell if they were busy filling orders for the resistance-tuned electronic measuring devices: "If the car was in the garage, there was no backlog. But if the car was parked in the driveway, business was good." Walt Disney Studios placed their first big order—for nine audio oscillators for sound production of the movie *Fantasia*.

Another propitious event of the era was a decision by the National Advisory Committee on Aeronautics to set up NACA's second field laboratory on the West Coast. At Ames Research Center adjoining Moffett Field, ground was broken late in 1939. Its initial research facilities, including several wind tunnels, were dedicated in the spring of 1940.

Hewlett - Packard's first structure — "The Redwood Building"

At Stanford, meanwhile, the klystron stepped up microwave research. Terman directed Edward Ginzton and other electrical engineering graduate students to assist Hansen in klystron improvement, for which Sperry had given Stanford $10,000. Before relocating with his physics team to Sperry's Long Island facility, Hansen taught a special class on the klystron for Terman's graduate students, creating a new generation of trained microwave engineers and preparing them for war work.

1935
Amelia Earhart leaves Honolulu on first solo flight across the Pacific.

In the Soviet Union, Stalin sends millions to harsh prison labor camps.

1936
Civil War in Spain; (1936-39).

1937
Italy, Germany, and Japan form an anticommunist pact.

1938
Lisa Meither and Hehn and Fritz Strassman coin the term "atomic fission".

1939
German troops invade Poland. World War II begins; (1939-45).

The first jet aircraft flies.

The Palo Alto garage where HP began is a California landmark now, "the birthplace of Silicon Valley"

On New Year's Day 1939 David Packard and William R. Hewlett tossed a coin in a rented Palo Alto garage to decide the order of names for their new company. They had started their business months earlier, with $538 and a few product ideas. In 1995, Hewlett-Packard Company is one of the world's technology leaders, with revenues approaching $30 billion, nearly 100,000 employees, and operations spanning the globe.

The Depression gripped America in 1934 when Packard and Hewlett, classmates in Frederick E. Terman's radio engineering program at Stanford University, neared graduation. As Packard tells it, "Bill and I had said if we can't get a job ourselves we'll just start our own company. ... Fred encouraged us to do that."

Before HP started, however, Packard accepted a position with General Electric in Schenectady, N.Y. Hewlett did graduate study at Massachusetts Institute of Technology and then with Terman where he developed a resistance-tuned oscillator. Their business start marked time until Terman brought Packard back to Stanford on a graduate fellowship. In 1938, they began part-time work in the garage behind Dave and Lucile Packard's home.

Soon, Walt Disney ordered eight HP200B oscillators for the movie *Fantasia*—HP's first big sale. By 1942 the company had built a plant in Palo Alto. It was still a small operation when World War II, as Hewlett put it, "changed everything." The Army Signal Corps called Hewlett to duty; Packard ran HP as it moved into war work, making audio oscillators used in proximity fuzes and microwave-signal generators used in radar and counterradar measures.

An incentive plan allowing employees to share in earnings enabled HP to keep a strong workforce despite wartime wage controls; later it became the basis for today's profit-sharing plan. Other "people-centered" practices followed as the founders fostered a work environment that aimed for innovation and achievement, promoted trust in people and teamwork, and rewarded employees for HP's success.

In 1947, the year HP incorporated, revenues topped $1.5 million. Three years later, when the Korean War began and electronics production soared, the company had in place an expanded line of test equipment including microwave and high-frequency products. In 1957, HP had its first public stock offering and began manufacturing at its new site in Stanford Research Park, near HP's current corporate offices.

Soon HP grew its product offerings through a series of acquisitions, all within its focused field of interest — electronics manufacturing. HP pursued new opportunities in data printing, medical electronics, and analytical instrumentation in the United States and in international markets with a manufacturing plant in Böblingen, West Germany, and marketing operations in Geneva, Switzerland.

In 1966, HP Laboratories—today among the world's leading electronics labs—formed as the company's central research facility. HP's first computer, designed as a controller for test and measuring instruments, was introduced in 1966.

In 1970, recession hit. Rather than reduce its workforce, HP instituted a temporary 10% hours-and-pay reduction. Everyone contributed to the necessary cost savings. A year later, the normal "flex-time" workweek resumed. Despite adverse economic trends, HP continued to develop new technologies and products, tightening its belt rather than incurring long-term debt.

The slide rule, once the tool of every engineer, slid into obsolescence after HP introduced the first scientific handheld calculator in 1972. Also in 1972, the company ventured into business computing with the HP 3000 minicomputer.

After sales passed $1 billion in 1976, the founders again showed their willingness to delegate responsibility. John Young became president in 1977 and chief executive officer in 1978, supported by three executive vice presidents. Bill and Dave remained on the board of directors.

Focusing on innovation and quality, HP stayed a steady, profitable course, as it introduced its first personal computer for technical users in 1980. Yokogawa Hewlett-Packard of Tokyo, Japan, a joint venture formed in 1963, won the prestigious Deming Prize for quality in 1982.

The new management team had its hands full during the 1980s, a time of increasing global competition and rapid change. Young led HP's success in the

In 1939, David Packard (seated) and William R. Hewlett produced an innovative audio oscillator.

Dave Packard and Bill Hewlett (right) at the landmark dedication in 1989, their company's 50th anniversary year

computer business. He also ousted the "not-invented-here" syndrome, contending that HP need not do everything itself but could use supplier alliances while capitalizing on its key strengths.

In 1984, HP helped create a new market for fast, inexpensive printing with the debut of the Thinkjet printer and the LaserJet printer, HP's most successful product ever. The next year, an epic R&D effort gave birth to an industry-leading family of Precision Architecture computer systems.

Bill Hewlett retired as a director in 1987, and Dave Packard relinquished his board chairmanship in 1993. Through separate family philanthropic foundations, both founders have been benefactors of educational, scientific, and health-care institutions.

Lewis E. Platt succeeded Young as president and CEO in 1992. By 1995, the company had sold more than 30 million printers. Today most of its revenue comes from a wide range of computer and computer-related products and services. HP's 23,000 products also include electronic test and measurement instruments and systems, networking products, medical electronic equipment, instruments and systems for chemical analysis, handheld calculators, and electronic components.

More than two-thirds of its revenues are generated abroad—principally in Europe. HP manufacturing and research centers are widely dispersed in Europe, Asia Pacific, Latin America, Canada and more than two dozen U.S. locations. Sales support through 600 sales offices or independent distributorships serve more than 120 countries.

Heavy investment in research and development (typically about 9% of annual net revenue), coupled with an ability to manufacture and market leading-edge technology quickly, feeds HP's steady flow of useful new products.

HP is widely recognized for a company culture known as "the HP way," once described by Bill Hewlett as "the policies and actions that flow from the belief that men and women want to do a good job, a creative job, and that if they are provided with the proper environment they will do so. Closely coupled with this is the HP tradition of treating each individual with consideration and respect, and recognizing individual achievements." Related values include uncompromising integrity, emphasis on teamwork to achieve common objectives, and encouraging flexibility and innovation.

Practices based on those values and objectives include "management by objectives" in which all employees set goals they intend to achieve; "management by walking around," which brings managers into frequent contact with individuals and groups; a decentralized organization with decision-making pushed to the lowest possible level; and avoiding

business opportunities that could lead to a "hire and fire" work environment.

Technological possibilities over the next 50 years are likely to dwarf those of the past 50. For example, the merging of measurement, computation, and communication technologies is revolutionizing the way people gather and share information. Emerging global networks and specialized digital-information products will enable people to communicate quickly and easily using text, graphics, audio, or video.

HP's expertise is helping create and manage these data highways and produce products that let people plug into the networks. The company's diverse capabilities set it apart from others that provide either computers or instruments, but not both.

HP intends to continue as a leading contributor to education and other important human needs in its communities. Citizenship is a long-held HP priority, as relevant to the company as profits.

The garage where it all began is now California's registered historical landmark No. 976— the "birthplace of Silicon Valley." Bill and Dave's legacy of humanistic management still thrives. Even as Hewlett-Packard Company embraces the rich heritage of the past, the company speeds into a future full of opportunities.

When Bill Hewlett (left) returned from WWII Army duty , he and Dave Packard put HP into microwave measurement

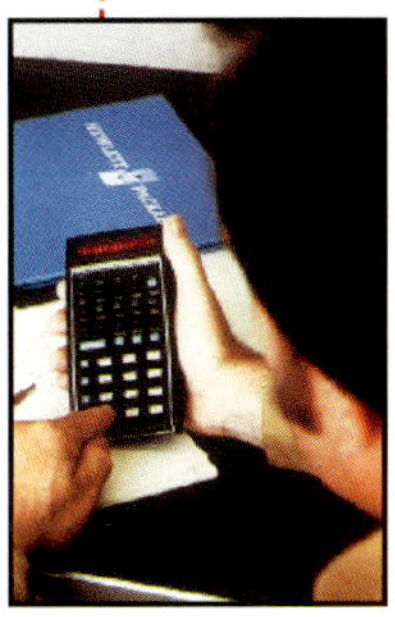

The first scientific hand-held calculator, introduced by HP in 1972, quickly wooed engineers away from slide rules

1940
Radar is developed.

1941
The U.S. enters World War II after Japanese attack on U.S. fleet in Pearl Harbor, Hawaii.

Sir Alexander Fleming discovers penicillin.

1942
The Western Allies sign an anti-Axis pact Jan. 1.

The first nuclear reactor is activated.

The world's first computer (ENIAC) is created.

The U.S. defeats Japan in sea battle near Midway Island in the Pacific.

1943
The aqualung is invented.

Dinah's Shack restaurant, Palo Alto (circa 1947)

Chapter 6: World War II Brings Science-Based Weapons to the Fore

Nazi Germany's shock troops, employing blitzkrieg tactics, had overrun most of Western Europe. Japan's forces, meanwhile, were rampaging through large parts of Asia. Most Americans believed the United States would have to fight.

In 1940, the British Royal Air Force and the German Luftwaffe were locked in the aerial battle of Britain. Despite the cruel punishment its people and cities were taking, Britain had a secret edge. It had developed radar, and the advent of the klystron — light enough to be put aboard aircraft — would later make the British system more workable. It arrived too late for employment in the air defense of Britain, but in time to help quell the menace of Nazi submarines. This technology symbolized the new science-based weapons the war was bringing to the fore, and it greatly aided Britain in beating off the U-boat assaults.

Under President Franklin Roosevelt's leadership, the United States supplied war materials to Britain and also to the Soviet Union after Germany turned on that former ally. America's scientists and engineers were mustered for an all-out effort to develop new weapons.

In December 1941, Japan bombed U.S. forces at Pearl Harbor with devastating effect, and attacked American and British bases in the Far East. Within days Congress declared the United States at war with Japan, Germany, and Italy.

Varians brothers with klystron

Companies along the San Francisco Peninsula quickly shifted from a preparedness to a war footing. Eitel-McCullough and Litton Engineering Laboratories geared up to produce vacuum tubes in unprecedented quantities. Kaar Engineering became a leading builder of two-way radios. Dalmo Victor developed military airborne radar equipment. Lenkurt built microwave telephone systems. In San Jose, Food Machinery and Chemical Corp., long a fabricator of agricultural spray pumps and cannery machinery, shifted operations to become a leading producer of tracked military vehicles.

Fred Terman at Stanford answered the call of his old MIT mentor, Vannevar Bush, to head the top-secret Radio Research Laboratory at Harvard University, eventually leading a corps of 800 scientists and engineers. The Army Signal Corps ordered Bill Hewlett to active duty again, this time for the duration. Dave Packard managed their company's defense production after 1942, in the first plant Hewlett-Packard built on Page Mill Road.

Terman's lab personnel devised jamming devices, particularly a radar countermeasure known as chaff, and developed tunable receivers for detecting and analyzing radar signals. Some of the related manufacturing was assigned to HP, which also made proximity fuzes that

Hewlett-Packard's first post-garage shop

had only to be shot near, not strike, an enemy tank or plane to score a hit. These fuzes gave the Allies an edge in both the air war and tank clashes like the Battle of the Bulge. The sophisticated radar countermeasures HP worked on were not completed by the war's end in August 1945, but they were ready when the Cold War began soon afterward. Atomic weapons dropped by the United States on Hiroshima and Nagasaki hastened Japan's surrender without the necessity to assault her homeland — an operation deemed likely to cause up to a million more U.S. casualties.

Clearly America's gamble on science-based weapons had paid off by helping the Allies to win the war and, despite the terrible costs of the conflict in lives and treasure, shortening its duration and reducing casualties.

While doing war work in the East, Terman, Hansen, the Varian brothers, Edward Ginzton and others learned from personal experience how Harvard and MIT managed their relations with Washington and how defense production firms such as Sperry operated. They acquired a taste for large-scale, project-oriented science. Stanford University had not played such a role in the long, grinding years of war. Many of its faculty had scattered, although one who remained on campus, physics Professor Paul Kirkpatrick, had developed the X-ray microscope in 1945. When peace finally came, it brought eagerness to reorganize for a new era — along with turbulence and shortages.

Terman was named dean of engineering in 1944, many months before he could return West. When he finally did come home, he had important new concepts in mind. He foresaw a rising tide of U.S. government support for science and technology, owing to their wartime successes. And he was convinced that his own field, electronics, was due to become even more essential in modern civilization. The Peninsula's World War II role in microwave tube production for radio and radar clearly was destined for further expansion, after a rocky readjustment to peacetime conditions.

University Ave., Palo Alto

An early signal of a fresh outlook on campus was the founding of Stanford Research Institute in 1946. SRI was created to do applied and contract research in conjunction with the university, with leading California businesses and industries among its sponsors. High hopes for this not-for-profit enterprise were not misplaced, for among SRI's accomplishments in subsequent years were such quantum jumps as magnetic ink character recognition (1955), ink-jet printing (1961), optical disk recording (1963), the mouse computer input device (1964), and the acoustic coupler/modem (1965). Companies hungry to develop these better mousetraps beat a path to SRI's doors in Menlo Park.

1945

The U.S. drops the atomic bomb on Japanese cities of Hiroshima and Nagasake.

Nazis report the death of Adolf Hitler.

Italian patriots execute Mussolini.

Germany surrenders to the Allies ending the war in Europe.

Percy Spencer invents the microwave oven in the U.S.

The forty year cold war between the U.S. and the Soviet Union begins.

1946

The United Nations General Assembly meets for the first time.

Reynold Johnson headed the IBM team that invented random-access disk storage

Since opening its first facility in the Santa Clara Valley in 1943, International Business Machines (IBM) has provided much more than jobs to what has become known as "Silicon Valley." For over 50 years, IBM San Jose has consistently made a significant contribution to the local economy–to the civic, ecological, cultural, health, and educational well-being of the community–as well as to the field of computer technology, in general.

Shortly after IBM established its first manufacturing facility in San Jose, California, a punch plant converted from a former laundry, the company donated $5,000 to the Community Chest. As the company continued to expand, so, too, have its donations of money, equipment, and its most valuable resource–people. Several San Jose IBM employees have taken a full year's leave with full pay to work in various community service projects, as well as on faculties in predominantly minority schools. In 1990, IBM San Jose and its employees gave more than $6 million in community support to the Santa Clara Valley United Way.

The company has invested more than $50 million in a decade-long groundwater protection program in San Jose. To help combat the area's drought, IBM San Jose has invested over $5.7 million in an air and steam stripping facility that recycles groundwater. With an aggressive program to eliminate the use of chlorofluorcarbons (CFCs), IBM San Jose reduced its emissions more than 90 percent and has committed to eliminating the use of CFCs in manufacturing worldwide.

Today, IBM San Jose's economic impact on Santa Clara County has surpassed $1 billion, which includes salaries, taxes, supplies, services, utilities, and other business expenditures. As important as its economic and civic contributions, however, is IBM San Jose's role in establishing Silicon Valley as the world's leading technology center.

IBM San Jose is the birthplace of one of the most important innovations in the computer industry–disk storage. In 1952, IBM established a major research laboratory on Notre Dame Avenue, in San Jose, to develop a new storage technology. At the time, data was stored in one of three ways–magnetic tape reels, core arrays, and drums–and IBM's 6,000 U.S. customers were using up to 16 billion punched cards annually on 100,000 rented machines. Company engineers canvassed customers and learned that there was a demand for computers. Although the computer had been invented in the East Coast, most of the early users of computers–in government and the aeronautical industry–as well as a vast reservoir of digital engineering talent, were in the San Francisco Bay Area. Unable to persuade electronics engineers to leave the weather and lifestyle of the Golden State for New York, IBM decided to move the mountain to Mohammed.

So, in 1952, gifted inventor Reynold Johnson, father of the test-scoring machine that for decades spared educators the tedium of hand-grading exams, was sent to San Jose to head the new lab. He, two assistants, and 50 locally hired engineers began to investigate methods of storing large quantities of information in a form that would enable any portion of the data to be available to a central processor in milliseconds. Among the forces driving this development in computer technology was IBM customer Zellerbach Paper Company, which, along with other enterprising business customers, recognized that they needed random access (though they didn't call it that) to their master files. The result, four years later, was the 305 RAMAC (Random Access Method of Accounting and Control)–and the birth of the Direct Access Storage Device (DASD) industry. In 1984, the American Society of Mechanical Engineers designated RAMAC an International Historic Mechanical Engineering Landmark, and in 1986, Johnson, then a retired IBM Fellow, received the National Medal of Technology from President Reagan. Today, disk storage is the dominant medium for on-line storage in all computers, from mainframes, to desktops, to notebooks.

In 1956, the General Products Division (GPD) opened in south San Jose to manufacture the RAMAC and to continue DASD development. In 1962, IBM San Jose introduced removable disk packs, each capable of holding two million characters. The "floppy" disks used in the first generation of small computers originated in San Jose. In 1973, IBM San Jose introduced the "Winchester" disk technology that set industry standards for heads, disks, and head-disk assemblies for the next decade. The company also was the first to use thin-film recording heads, which led to significant advances in disk storage capabilities.

RAMAC, the direct access storage device invented in San Jose, is an International Historic Engineering Landmark

The IBM 305 RAMAC originally was 6 feet tall and weighed thousands of pounds

Disk technology is but one of many innovations that have come from IBM San Jose. Others include the IBM 609 Card Calculator; the IBM 1620 Data Processing System; the trillion bit file, the IBM Photodigital Storage System; the IBM 1500 computer-assisted instructional system; the IBM 1130 Computing System; the IBM 3614 Consumer Transaction System; and the IBM 3800 Printing Subsystem (a non-impact printer combining laser technology, clcctrophotograph, and microprogrammed control, which revolutionized computer output).

Other innovations credited to the San Jose group include the "Shoebox," a voice-activated adding machine; the automated teller machine (ATM); "Scamp," one of the first portable computers; bar coding; relational data bases; and magnetic stripe technology such as that used on credit cards.

The IBM PC, introduced in 1981, scored with business users and soon had imitators

In 1976, the Santa Teresa Laboratory, IBM's first facility built specifically for programmers, was opened on Bailey Road, San Jose, followed by the Almaden Research Center, on Bernal Road, San Jose, a decade later. Dedicated to pure and applied research, Almaden is one of only three IBM Research Divisions worldwide. IBM also maintains sales and service offices throughout the Santa Clara Valley, a scientific center in Palo Alto, California, and a facility dedicated to federal government projects in Sunnyvale, California.

IBM San Jose, part of the Storage Systems Products Division (SSPD), today has responsibility for worldwide development and U.S. manufacturing of high-end direct access storage devices (DASD). The site is also responsible for the development of DASD attachments and controllers; the development of high-end storage systems software; and the manufacture of high-end tape drives developed at IBM's Tuscon, Arizona, laboratory. Now as during the past five decades, this group of IBMers–some 9,000-plus strong, in 50 buildings throughout the Bay Area–continues to make their mark on the community of Silicon Valley and on society at large, with their tremendous innovations and contributions.

2.5-inch disk drive stores 100 times more data, is 45 times faster, and costs 10,000 times less than original RAMAC

Experts from numerous fields bring their talents to bear at the SRI Laboratory

Little did the small band of industry leaders and scholars who, in the early 1920s, envisioned a West Coast research center know that their vision would become one of the largest, most prestigious contract research institutions in the world. Unfortunately, though strongly supported by such luminary figures as Stanford alumnus Herbert Hoover, the hoped-for San Francisco Bay Area research institute would be delayed for another 20 years due to the Great Depression and World War II.

In 1946, however, the time and conditions were finally right to bring the vision to reality, and Stanford Research Institute (SRI) was founded by Stanford University in conjunction with a group of western U.S. business executives as a nonprofit organization with close ties to the university. The research center was the brainchild of "the three musketeers"–Dr. Robert E. Swain, Dr. Philip A. Leighton, and H. Dudley Swim of Stanford University–who laid the early groundwork. Dr. Alvin C. Eurich, former acting Stanford president, is credited with being the "architect" of SRI. Legendary Northern California businessman Antholl McBean is considered SRI's founder and remained a lifetime proponent of the institute. The "pilot" and second director, J.E. (Jesse) Hobson, provided the 1948 kickstart and resultant momentum that fueled SRI's rapid and continued growth.

SRI was launched on a shoestring in borrowed space at Stanford University with a basic purpose to apply science for useful purposes. Initially dedicated primarily to supporting economic stability in the western region of the United States, SRI's focus soon became national and then international in scope.

When SRI opened its doors in 1946, the American economy had just begun its war-to-peacetime transformation, and an ambitious wave of industry had begun to swell, much of it aimed at the West Coast. The 1940s and 1950s were a time of accelerated industrial and economic growth for the nation, and an exciting era in research and development. It was also the beginning of what has become a highly competitive, technologically advanced global economy. During a 1949 meeting with President Harry Truman regarding an Air Force-sponsored SRI project, Truman responded to news of SRI's plans to expand abroad with an enthusiastic, "...the world needs SRI. Push ahead; don't hesitate!"

SRI's first project, conducted at government labs in Salinas, California, consisted of a joint effort with the university's genetics department to develop the Guayule plant as a source of rubber. The next project was a study in aircraft production for the U.S. Air Force. During the '40s and '50s, SRI made numerous contributions to both the "hard" and "soft" (economics, management research) sciences. SRI did pioneering work in techno-economics, the management sciences, and electronics. Early projects included evaluating and perfecting the nation's civilian defense program, geophysical exploration in Alaska, a feasibility study for Disneyland, and the development of "hydracushion" boxcars, a 100-ton amphibious barge, solar collectors, and magnetic check scanners. The institute also tackled the smog and air pollution problems, examined the status and future of the forestry products industry, and executed a study of the world's longest pipeline.

In the early 1950s, SRI conducted its first major overseas projects, which included a techno-economic field study on the Babassu nut industry in Brazil, an economics study in Cuba, and a study of Italy's mechanical industries. Its involvement with international government and corporate research communities continues to this day, from Russia's Academy of Sciences to Japan's Ministry of International Trade and Industry (MITI).

As SRI grew and added brilliant scientists and researchers from around the country (and eventually, from around the world) as staff members, the institute quickly outgrew the first offices in the Physics corner of the Main Quad at Stanford. In 1947, SRI moved to the main building of the former Dibble General Hospital at Stanford Village in Menlo Park. Named after a World War II Army general, the hospital was used to treat soldiers, and later to house Stanford students. As SRI continued to grow, it expanded into one building after another of Stanford Village. Several new labs were added, including a television lab, an electronics facility, an ion exchange lab, a gauge lab, an air/water pollution complex, and an analytical service facility for chemistry and physics.

Finally, in 1958, the institute purchased the property from the government and continued to develop or convert buildings into state-of-the-science research facilities. That year, SRI built its first building on what had once been the estate of Timothy Hopkins, a prominent West Coast business executive, taking care to leave Mr. Hopkins' prized oak trees in place. A milestone in the history of SRI came in 1969 with the opening of its International Building, which has become known as the House of All the Lands, based on the ancient Chinese proverb, "From a house of all the lands comes understanding among people."

Throughout its nearly 50-year history, SRI has received strong support from government, scientific, and business leaders from around the globe. Principal speakers at SRI conferences and events have include such dignitaries as David Rockefeller, Malcolm Forbes, and Richard Nixon. Local supporters, many of whom served on SRI's board, have included prominent Bay Area citizens and business executives such as David Packard, S.D. Bechtel Sr., and J.D. Zellerbach.

In 1970, SRI separated from Stanford and became an independent nonprofit contract research and consulting firm. Although it changed its name to SRI International in 1977, SRI has continued to maintain close ties with Stanford, as well as with many leading universities in the world.

Today, SRI employs approximately 2,700 people and has annual revenues in excess of $300 million. In addition to the headquarters, R&D facilities, and specialized laboratories in Menlo Park, SRI also operates offices throughout the world. In 1987, SRI acquired the David Sarnoff Research Center, a wholly owned for-profit subsidiary, formerly the corporate research center for RCA and considered the world's premier television research organization.

Contract research and development continues to be the institute's mainstay, but SRI also helps develop and commercialize products, build prototypes, and offer technology/management consulting services. Significant SRI contributions to technology and science include ink-jet printing, the "mouse" computer device, "windows" computer technology, packet-switched radio systems, Halofantrine anti-malarial drug, laser retinal photocoagulator, optical disk recording, Edatrexate lung cancer drug, and many more. Today, SRI maintains over 100 labs, ranging from those focusing on artificial intelligence to biochemical engineering, environmental chemistry, computer technology, and health care.

Though both the world and the institute have changed considerably since 1946, SRI has remained dedicated to its founding mission, as inscribed on a stone set in front of the institute's International Building: "Dedicated to the peace and prosperity of mankind" –through the advancement and application of science and technology.

SRI International provides clients around the world with expertise to manage their businesses in today's technology-driven marketplace

Hoover Tower dominates Stanford U. Skyline

1947

Independence of India.

Dead Sea Scrolls discovered.

1948

The Berlin Airlift; (1948-49).

A Hindu fanatic assassinates Mohandas K. (Mahatma) Gandhi.

The transistor is invented.

Israeli independence leads to the first Arab-Israeli War.

1949

The U.S. and West European nations form the North Atlantic Treaty Organization (NATO) for collective security.

Chapter 7: Postwar Era Ushers in Federal Support for University Research

Frederick Terman returned to Stanford University as dean of engineering in 1946. His belief that science and technology would gain new infusions of government support as a result of their wartime successes was soon borne out. Within a few months, the Office of Naval Research awarded Stanford a $225,000 annual contract for basic research.

This funding empowered Terman to shape new research plans. He set up three projects. The one in physics led to the discovery of nuclear magnetic resonance and the Nobel Prize for Felix Bloch in 1952 — the first in a long string of high honors for Stanford scientists. The chemistry project fizzled, but the electronics project led to creation of Stanford's Electronics Research Laboratories and, soon, a plan for developing a Stanford Linear Accelerator Center.

Edward Ginzton at Varian

Russell and Sigurd Varian returned to the Bay Area in 1948 after their wartime stint with Sperry at Long Island, N.Y. Soon they joined Edward Ginzton, Marvin Chodorow, and other Sperry colleagues in forming Varian Associates. Initially the firm settled in San Carlos, where Sperry had had a prewar outpost. In addition to producing klystrons, Varian Associates developed applications of the linear accelerator and nuclear induction devices W.W. Hansen had pioneered at Stanford. Hansen mortgaged his house to give the company a just-in-time loan, and died soon afterward.

Initial Varian Associates products were based directly on Stanford-owned patents, and many of the associates were also Stanford faculty members. These close interties prompted Varian to seek a base closer to the university, and in 1950 the firm took the first lease of Stanford land designated for light industry, moving operations there in 1952-53.

Soon after World War II ended, scientists at Ames Research Center turned their attention to understanding problems of high-speed flight. One outgrowth of this effort was the concept by Robert T. Jones of using swept-back wings. Later H. Julian Allen and Alfred J. Eggers Jr. developed the blunt-body concept for ballistic missiles and spacecraft re-entering Earth's atmosphere at tremendous velocities.

The Korean War began in mid-1950 and soon imparted a great surge to electronics industries. Poised for this growth with a full line of electronic measuring devices ready, Hewlett-Packard found its business and work force doubling every year. HP products were in high demand for electronics production and medical and military uses. Meanwhile, the war sent Office of Naval Research envoys straight to Fred Terman with a new proposal. Quickly, a new Applied Electronics Laboratory was built with Navy money and a gift from Hewlett-Packard. The lab ran on $450,000 a year in federal funding.

Early Hewlett-Packard employees assemble circuits

International Business Machines Corp., spurred by the Korean War, put its first large-scale electronic computer into production in New York State in 1952. Hoping to tap a new source of engineers in California, the company selected San Jose as home for a western research laboratory. Reynold Johnson, who had invented a test-scoring machine in 1937 and then managed IBM time clock and key punch developments, was assigned to head the project. Johnson and two assistants traveled west with a free hand to staff the new lab and choose what it would work on. Among the numerous projects begun in a former printing plant at 99 Notre Dame Avenue in San Jose, one entitled "Source Recording" moved to the fore. It was aimed to mechanize the handling of punched cards and eliminate awkward "tub files" that clerks had to staff. In fact, it ultimately reshaped the computer industry.

By early 1953, magnetic disks had been selected as the best medium for a random access memory. Digital magnetic recording was then primitive, and disks presented stability problems. An air head containing a magnetic read/write element met the need for constant head-to-surface spacing. To access stacked disks, IBM employed its first servo system. The RAMAC 305 made its debut in 1955, enabling businesses to process information right away rather than wait for a batch to pile up. Its disk file marked the birth of the direct access storage device industry. IBM set up a San Jose manufacturing plant, but kept the lab independent.

Meanwhile, on the small portion of Stanford lands earmarked for light industry, Eastman Kodak followed Varian as a tenant. This prompted Terman to object that Stanford ought not to host firms having no close relations with university purposes and research. His stand won him a role in the university's land development planning, and in 1953 the trustees junked a plan for extensive residential development and set up Stanford Industrial Park with over 650 choice acres to lease to high-technology enterprises.

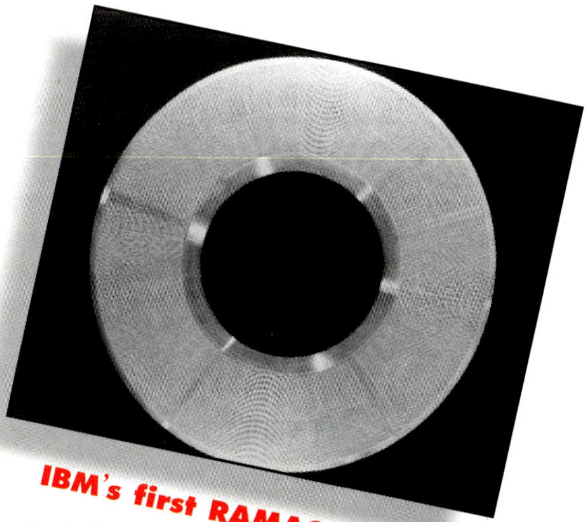

IBM's first RAMAC disk

The microwave tube era was still gathering momentum but a tiny device called the transistor was due to transform it. William Shockley had co-invented the transistor with John Bardeen and Walter Brattain at Bell Labs in 1947. Its first commercial use was in 1952 in a hearing aid. Soon afterward, transistors supplanted vacuum tubes in radios.

A epochal step in 1952 foreshadowed the advent of genetic engineering. Joshua Lederberg, then at the University of Wisconsin, discovered that viruses that attack bacteria can transmit genetic material from one bacterium to another.

1949
Albert Einstein states his theory of gravitation.

1950
Korean War; (1950-53).

Campaign for civil rights in the U.S. for African Americans; (1950s).

1952
A helicopter crosses the Atlantic for the first time.

The hydrogen bomb undergoes tests.

1953
Mao Zedong introduces the first five-year plan.

DNA is discovered.

E.P. Hillary of New Zealand and native guide Tenzing climb Mt. Everest, the world's highest mountain.

The White House and Air Force used this 1970 Dacom Securefax terminal

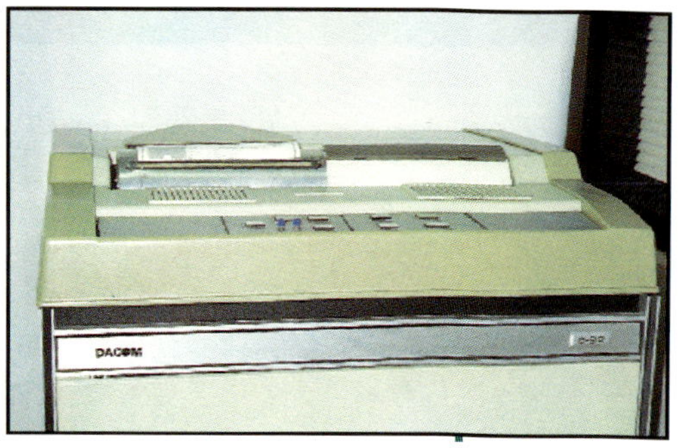

Ricoh Corporation, a billion dollar company in its own right, is a wholly owned subsidiary of the multinational Ricoh Company, Limited, with headquarters in Japan. Ricoh's presence in the United States dates back to 1962, and its roots in Silicon Valley date back to 1966 when a start-up company named Dacom Inc. began operations in Palo Alto.

Prior to 1969, the document facsimile industry was in its infancy. The throughput of fax terminals at that time was about eight minutes per page over the public-switched telephone network (PSTN). This made the use of fax terminals very inefficient and expensive.

In 1969 Dacom introduced a digital fax terminal utilizing their proprietary data compression technology that could transmit documents with a typical throughput of two minutes per page.

A second-generation fax terminal with a digital port designed to operate with external encryption/decryption equipment was developed by Dacom for the U.S. Air Force and the White House Communications Agency in 1970.

During the year 1970, Columbia Broadcasting System, now known as CBS, Inc., was seeking state-of-the-art technology that might have application to the television and broadcast industry. About the same time, Dacom (by then located in Sunnyvale) was seeking capital to finance their third-generation document fax development program.

Representatives of Dacom and CBS met and discussed further development possibilities utilizing Dacom's data compression technology. At that time, it was determined that data compression technology was too primitive to meet the demands of the television industry; however, it was recognized that development of a digital fax terminal with data compression could have a major impact on the infant fax industry. About this same time, Savin Business Machines Corporation, now known as Savin Corporation, became interested in marketing digital fax transceivers.

In the late months of 1970, a partnership, originally named Dicom but later changed to Rapifax Company, was formed by CBS and Savin to finance the development, tooling, manufacturing, and distribution of a sub-one-minute fax transceiver for use over the PSTN. These transceivers, designed for mass production, would be suitable for widespread use in business and government applications in many countries throughout the world. In December of 1970, the Savin/CBS partnership purchased the majority and controlling interest in Dacom and immediately initiated development of this new fax transceiver.

Rapifax also contracted with Ricoh Company, Ltd., of Japan to join the venture by participating in the development program with a view toward manufacturing the final product. Ricoh, as a major worldwide supplier of copier machines, utilized their expertise in the development of paper transport mechanisms, optical systems, and other electro-mechanical devices. Their proven ability to productize and mass-produce office automation equipment was also of critical importance.

Rapifax 100 facsimile transceiver sales were initiated early in 1974. Slightly earlier, in 1973, Dacom began marketing of the Series 400 terminals. Both terminals employed the same basic technology, but the Dacom models were modified for special applications.

Rapifax company needed additional financing in 1973 in order to produce and market the Rapifax 100 transceiver. This led to the incorporation of Rapifax with Ricoh Co., Ltd., purchasing the majority interest in the new corporation.

In January of 1977, Rapifax purchased the remaining shares of Dacom stock and in 1978 the companies were merged to form Rapicom, Inc. CBS and Savin sold their interests in the company to Ricoh, and Rapicom became a wholly owned subsidiary of Ricoh Co., Ltd.

For several years Rapicom concentrated on further development of fax transceivers and, of course,

In 1973, Dacom (now part of Ricoh) modified Series 400 fax terminals for special applications distribution of the standard fax products coming out of Japan and the special application products manufactured in Silicon Valley. However, in 1984, Rapicom and Ricoh of America, Inc., were merged to form Ricoh Corporation, a supplier of copiers, fax, computer peripherals, other office automation products, and some consumer electronic products.

In 1979, Ricoh opened a research facility in San Jose called Ricoh Systems Inc. (RSI). While their interests were in office product technologies in general, their primary efforts were directed toward copier technology initially.

In 1987, RSI was absorbed into Ricoh Corporation as an operating division. In December 1989, the division moved into Menlo Park facilities and became known as the Ricoh California Research Center. The center's interests are more diversified today; its personnel perform research in such areas as artificial intelligence, neural networks, pattern recognition, information retrieval techniques, color compression, and secure systems applications.

The merger/acquisition timeline described above is most important to the understanding of Ricoh's Silicon Valley roots. However, in addition to the standard commercial fax products developed by Dacom and Rapicom in the 1970s, three special-application fax products were developed that are particularly noteworthy:

1. Dacom 300 Series Fax System (1972-1992)—This was a very high resolution system with broadcast and error detection/correction capability which could transmit a full-size newspaper page in about 4.5 minutes simultaneously to multiple reception sites. The received image was output on photographic film from which printing plates could be etched. Many of these systems, capable of color reproduction, were installed worldwide; the largest such network is used to print the *USA Today* newspaper. This system was produced and sold for 20 years until the technology was sold to a third party.

2. Weatherfax (circa 1974-1984)—This was a special fax system developed for the U.S. National Weather Service. Utilizing proprietary data compression algorithms customized for the transmission of 11- by 17-inch weather maps via leased lines or satellite circuits, this system was also used by the Air Force. This product line was abandoned about 1984, although royalties were still received until 1992.

3. Secure fax (1972-present)—The Dacom 412 "Securefax" terminals were introduced into the Department of Defense in 1973. These terminals were designed for the transmission of classified documents in as little as 22 seconds per page. Through 1983 the Dacom and Rapicom share of the nontactical market was, arguably, 99%. With different technology and the introduction of competitors during the 1980s, Ricoh retains its market leadership with an estimated share of 75% through 1994.

Ricoh Corporation has approximately 150 employees in the Silicon Valley facilities. Kazuyuki (Ken) Baba is currently in charge of the System Products Development Division in San Jose, where most of the Silicon Valley employees are based. Dr. Peter Hart directs the Ricoh California Research Center in Menlo Park.

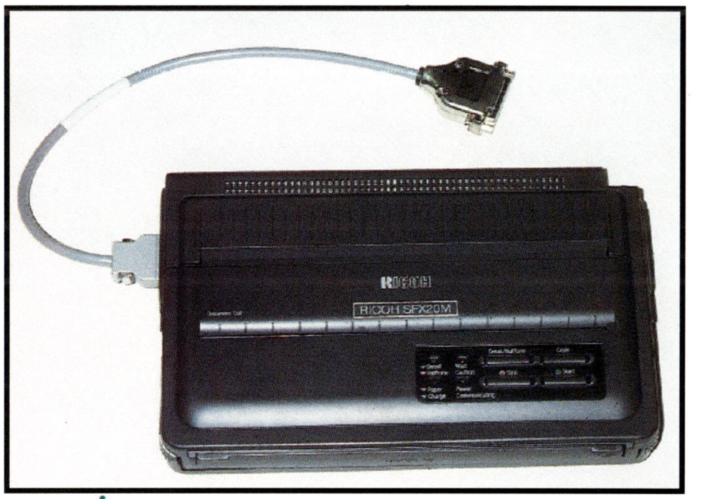

1994 Ricoh 6-pound terminal has document fax and encryption interface capability

Plaque explains first digital facsimile transceivers, introduced in 1974. Many remain in use.

Signetics, which in 1993 became part of Philips Semiconductors, was the first company in the world to be established for the exclusive purpose of developing, manufacturing, and distributing integrated circuits (ICs). More than 30 years after its founding, Philips continues to produce circuits for a wide range of applications, including multimedia, wireless communications, and audio/video.

The company was originally formed in September 1961 by a group of scientists and engineers working at legendary Fairchild Semiconductor. David Allison, David James, Lionel Kattner, and Mark Weisenstern were among the early pioneers of IC technology. Like Fairchild's founders before them, and a generation of entrepreneurs to come, they struck out on their own, calling their new company Signetics (a contraction of "Signal Network ICs").

The founders established their first facilities in Sunnyvale, California, where the company continues to maintain its headquarters for its U.S. operations. The company's worldwide headquarters are located in Eindhoven, The Netherlands.

Signetics was an early innovator in digital logic, with many of its logic circuits becoming industry standards. Within a year of its founding, the company's first family of bipolar digital diode transistor logic circuits had gained market acceptance and were finding initial application in military and space systems. Among the company's early innovations are the 555 timer, Dolby circuits, and the programmable read-only memory.

In November of 1962 Corning Glass Works purchased a majority interest in Signetics and became its parent company. Two years later the company designed and built its current main facility on East Arques Avenue.

Signetics grew quickly, eventually occupying 20 buildings and employing over 5,000 people locally. During its early years, all company operations, including manufacturing, R&D, and administration, were carried on in Sunnyvale.

Early assembly line workers check ICs with microscopes at Signetics (now Philips Semiconductors)

By the mid-1960s, the need to increase production levels compelled the company to establish its first off-site plant, in Provo, Utah. The Provo plant assembled military and space ICs and enabled Signetics to become the first IC company to receive both Minuteman approval (1967) and NASA line certification (1970). A fabrication plant was constructed in Orem, Utah, in 1969; it was later closed.

In 1966 the company established Signetics Korea Co., Ltd. ("Sig Kor") in Seoul, South Korea. The Sig Kor plant was the first low-cost production facility to both assemble and test ICs in the Far East. The company established its second Far Eastern assembly/ test plant in Bangkok, Thailand, in 1976.

In the early 1970s, then company president Charles Harwood initiated a revolutionary quality control program. And in 1985 Signetics became the first IC company to offer a "zero defects" warranty on all its products. That program, still actively implemented within Philips, has become an industry model.

By the mid-1970s Signetics had become a broad-based supplier of the major IC product lines and went public for a short while (1973-1975). In June 1975 the company was purchased by U.S. Philips Corporation, a wholly owned subsidiary of N.V. Philips of the Netherlands.

The company completed its Albuquerque, New Mexico, plant in 1982 and opened its Technology Center in Sunnyvale two years later.

Philips Semiconductors employs 1,250 people in Sunnyvale, headquarters for the North America Regional Sales Organization and two of the company's five business groups: the Automotive and Storage IC group and the Standard Products IC group. The Discrete Products Business Group was added in July 1994 and operates out of Slatersville, Rhode Island. The business groups develop, manufacture, and market their own products, and the sales organization is responsible for sales of all Philips Semiconductors products throughout North America.

The "name" partners in WSGR are, from left, John Goodrich, John Wilson, Larry Sonsini, and Mario Rosati

Silicon Valley has been the home of innovation for more than just the high technology and life sciences industries. By anticipating the enormous potential of young, entrepreneurial companies in the Valley and focusing on their most critical needs, Wilson, Sonsini, Goodrich & Rosati (WSGR) has become one of the most successful and influential law firms in the nation.

When the firm was founded in 1961, as McCloskey, Wilson & Mosher, legal business from the Valley's budding high-technology industry was flowing to the established, big-name law firms in San Francisco. Founding Partner John A. Wilson believed that a visionary Palo Alto firm could staunch that flow, and could grow in close partnership with local entrepreneurs. Wilson found a capable ally who came to share the same vision in Larry W. Sonsini, the first associate hired by the firm. During the late 1960s and early 1970s, Sonsini led the firm's efforts to forge lasting relationships with rising semiconductor and computer peripherals companies.

By 1978, when the firm began using its current name, it had established a reputation in the area of business most critical to the Valley's young, emerging companies: gaining access to the money they needed to finance their growth. Pete McCloskey had left to serve in Congress, and Roger Mosher had left to practice litigation in a smaller firm. Wilson (now retired but still active as "of counsel") and Sonsini (by then a leading partner of the firm) were joined on the masthead by John Goodrich and Mario Rosati. Goodrich specialized in international law, reflecting the increasingly sophisticated needs of the firm's clients. Rosati specialized in securities law (like Sonsini, he had been a protégé of Richard Jennings at the University of California's Boalt Hall in Berkeley) with a particular and ongoing interest in venture-backed start-ups.

Sonsini and his colleagues focused on assisting clients with initial public offerings (IPOs) of stock and on uniting promising entrepreneurs with the venture capital firms that, like WSGR, were growing in support of new industries born in the Valley. In the early 1980s, when the personal computer and software industries took off, WSGR was perfectly positioned. By representing companies like Coherent Inc., Apple Computer, and Novell Inc. in their IPOs, WSGR cemented its reputation as the nation's leading law firm for emerging growth, technology-based companies. WSGR's corporate personality had come to mirror that of its entrepreneurial clients, as reflected in a comment made by Al Shugart, the chief executive officer of Seagate Technology, about Larry Sonsini: "Larry's a combination lawyer, accountant, venture capitalist, and businessman."

WSGR has continued to grow by responding to the changing needs of successful entrepreneurs. For example, when shareholder class-action lawsuits began to proliferate in the 1980s, the firm built the nation's leading securities litigation defense capability for emerging growth companies. Later, WSGR built similar strengths for the key areas of intellectual property and antitrust litigation. As the life sciences industry blossomed, the firm established a dedicated group focused on the special needs of the biomedical and medical device companies.

Even as WSGR has profited by sharing the vision of its entrepreneurial clients, it has shared their values as well, by providing *pro bono* legal services to citizen and community groups throughout the state.

Today, with more than 275 lawyers and 1,000 clients, WSGR is firmly entrenched in the infrastructure of high technology and the life sciences, and also is the San Francisco Bay Area's most profitable law firm. By building its own organization based on long-term partnership with the Silicon Valley, WSGR now can offer a unique scalability in the full range of legal services as clients grow from the entrepreneurial start-up stage to the maturity of a *Fortune* 500 company.

Siliconix, Inc.

Richard J. Kulle, president and CEO of Siliconix

Siliconix was founded in 1962 as a manufacturer of junction field-effect transistors. In 1964, the company began production of field-effect transistors (FETs) using MOS (metallic-oxide semiconductor) technology. In 1968, Siliconix introduced the world's first analog switch integrated circuit (IC), and in 1970 the analog IC line was expanded with the addition of analog multiplexers.

The first commercially viable power MOSFET was introduced by Siliconix in 1975, and in 1984 the company combined its power MOSFET technology with CMOS IC technology to introduce a new line of power ICs.

In 1990, Richard E. Lee, one of Siliconix' original founders, retired as head of the company. Robert L. Wehrli replaced Lee as chairman of the board. Richard J. Kulle became president and chief executive officer in March 1990 and set in motion a plan to transform the company. By year-end 1994, revenue per employee had more than doubled.

Today, Siliconix continues to design and manufacture both power and analog semiconductor products. Siliconix power transistors and integrated circuits are mainly used for power management and motion control in computers, hard disk drives, automobiles, and telecommunications systems. The company's analog switches, multiplexers, and low-power transistors are used to sense, switch, and route signals in video, multimedia, instrumentation, and test equipment in both the industrial and hi-rel environments.

Siliconix provides products and technologies that directly answer the market's demand for smaller, more efficient, more cost-effective components. The company's LITTLE FOOT® discrete power transistors are compact solutions for motion control in hard disk drives and for load management in portable computers. These miniaturized products can be mounted directly to the printed circuit board; they are the first such power devices to be fully compatible with other surface-mounted components. LITTLE FOOT has also been designed into telecom systems, automotive air bag triggers, and other applications where space saving and efficiency are at a premium.

The company recently introduced an even smaller power MOSFET: the LITE FOOT® family. About half the size of LITTLE FOOT, LITE FOOT is designed for use in the most compact new electronic products, such as cellular telephones, personal digital assistants, hard disk drives, subnotebook computers, smart batteries, and PC Cards.

Siliconix power integrated circuits combine interface circuitry with power functions. A family of regulator and controller ICs designed for use with LITTLE FOOT discretes offers the optimal level of integration for DC-to-DC conversion in battery-operated equipment, including laptop and notebook computers. For data storage customers, the company has produced highly integrated chips for voice coil and spindle motor control. New products include power ICs for computers equipped with dual battery packs or PC Card slots, and power ICs for bus control in automobiles.

Santa Clara is the locale of corporate headquarters for Siliconix. The company's manufacturing includes wafer fabrication in Santa Clara, where a 4-inch wafer fab and a Class 1, 6-inch wafer fab are available, and high-volume assembly and testing in the company's facility in Taiwan, a joint venture in Shanghai, China, and subcontractors in the Philippines and India.

Siliconix is a member of the TEMIC Group, a microelectronics enterprise under the industrial leadership of AEG Daimler-Benz Industrie. TEMIC's Semiconductor Division includes Siliconix, Telefunken Semiconductors, Matra MHS, and Dialog Semiconductor. These companies now share their technologies and applications expertise, and take advantage of a combined international sales force.

Siliconix is a publicly traded company (NASDAQ:SILI). AEG Capital Corporation, headquartered in Basking Ridge, New Jersey, is the largest shareholder with 80.4% of the shares available as of December 31, 1994.

Workers at control stations oversee wafer fabrication at Santa Clara manufacturing facility

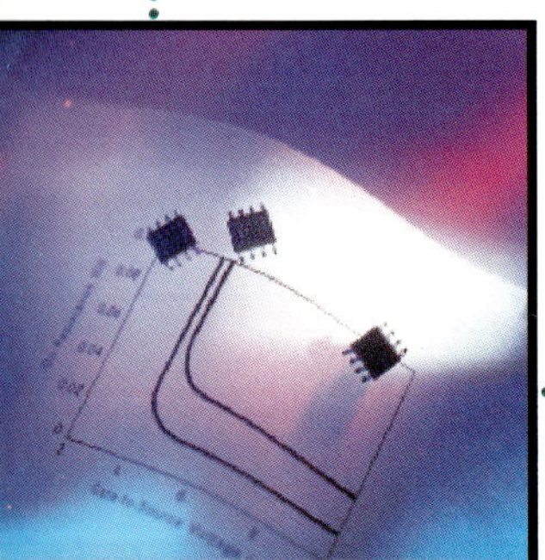

Advances in Siliconix's power transistors technologies are designed into the LITTLE FOOT family of small-outline power MOSFETs

Coherent, Inc.

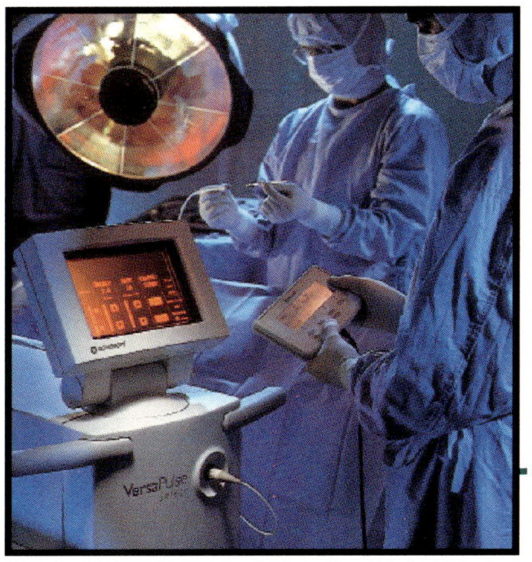

The Coherent VersaPulse® has become the laser of choice for arthroscopic procedures

Coherent's CO_2 UltraPulse® laser is widely used in cosmetic surgery

Coherent, Inc., the worldwide leader in lasers, has come a long way since it started in 1966 in the laundry room of a Palo Alto home. Physicist James L. Hobart and engineers Robert Rorden and Wayne Mefferd, three of the four technical cofounders, remain very active contributors as the company approaches its 30th anniversary. Their start-up team developed a unique carbon dioxide (CO_2) laser in just four months.

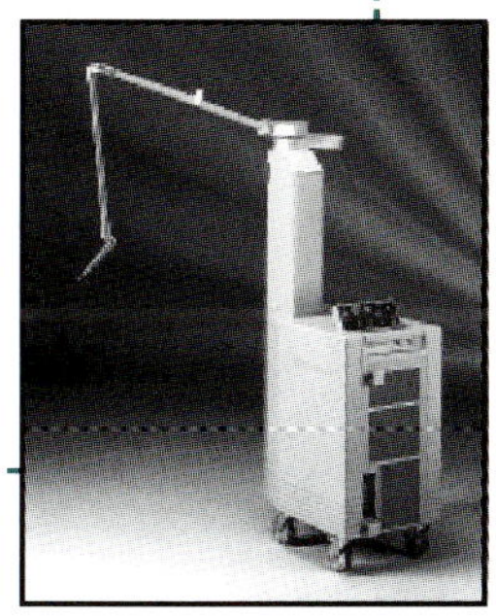

Why a laundry room? It had the only 220-volt electrical outlet available. The carbon dioxide laser was the first with a very high power output. While Hobart installed the first one sold, at the Boeing Co. in January 1967, he recalls, he burned a hole in a sport coat hanging nearby, and had to buy the owner a new one. This incident necessitated developing an instrument to measure the laser's power; this basic power meter is still manufactured today.

Hobart, currently chairman of the board and chief executive officer, has held top executive posts since the beginning. Henry E. Gauthier, who joined the company in January 1973, is president and chief operating officer.

In 1968 Coherent introduced an improved argon/krypton ion laser capable of producing high-power visible light. One-fifth the size and half the cost of competing products, it doubled revenues and led to the company's first profitable quarter. Coherent entered international markets with new financing provided by local investors led by Franklin (Pitch) Johnson. (Originally the founders—some of them former Spectra-Physics and Varian Associates employees—had anted $10,000, after which investments by DuPont and the Rockefeller family kept them eating.)

In 1969, the company entered the medical field—today the source of nearly half its revenues—with an argon photocoagulator, developed in conjunction with Stanford Research Institute and Drs. Christian Zweng and Hunter Little of the Palo Alto Medical Clinic. Coherent's eye-surgery lasers became a standard tool for ophthalmologists treating the three leading causes of blindness: glaucoma, diabetic retinopathy, and secondary cataracts. Today, Coherent systems are used in more than 20 minimally invasive surgical procedures, including cosmetic surgery for wrinkle removal.

Coherent went public (NASDAQ:COHR) in 1970. The next year it began making acquisitions, consolidated operations in Stanford Industrial Park, and developed a tunable jet stream dye laser.

In 1981, Coherent acquired Lambda Physik in West Germany, which has since contributed many advances in excimer lasers for scientific, medical, and micromachining applications.

Sales topped the $100 million mark in 1984, the year Coherent entered the ultrafast spectroscopy market. Ion lasers, originally confined to scientific research, were finding new industrial and medical applications in compact-disk mastering, direct imaging, and semiconductor processing.

Coherent manufactures a highly diversified selection of lasers: argon and krypton ion, carbon dioxide, diode, diode-pumped solid-state, dye, erbium, excimer, holmium, KTP, Nd:YAG, and titanium:sapphire. Its 150-plus products—lasers, laser systems, precision optics, and components—range in price from $500 to $500,000. The company is known for employing numerous engineers and physicists and investing more than 11% of sales annually in research that yields about 40 new products each year.

Coherent's headquarters and laser group are now in Santa Clara. Its medical group is in Palo Alto, with components, optics, and instruments manufactured in Auburn. Other locations are in seven overseas nations. Sales revenues, $215 million in 1994, rose sharply in early 1995 quarters—as did Coherent's prospects

Proud papas celebrate creating the first high-power CO_2 laser in just four months. Coherent CEO James Hobart is at right.

Chapter 10: Inside the Atom, Outside Earth's Atmosphere

1964
U.S. Civil Rights Act bans racial discrimination in federal funding and employment.

Chemotherapy treatment for illness, particularly cancer, is developed.

1965
Vietnam War; U.S. intervention ends in humiliating withdrawal of U.S. troops; (1965-75).

Malcolm X, African-American Muslim leader and activist, is shot and killed.

Watts Riots in Los Angeles, California.

Cultural Revolution in China.

During the mid-1960s, two federally funded Peninsula facilities pushed research deep into the atom and far beyond Earth's airy envelope. Other trends of the era included the buildup of a world-class medical center, moves to the south by burgeoning semiconductor firms, and the arrival of a major biotechnology company.

Syntex at work

Syntex Corporation, which had been founded in Mexico, opened a research lab in Stanford Industrial Park in 1964. Soaring on the popularity of the birth control pill it introduced that year, Syntex added production space. Carl Djerassi, principal developer of the pill, joined the Stanford chemistry faculty. Syntex research director Alejandro Zaffaroni in 1968 founded Alza Corporation, which offered skin patches and other new drug delivery methods.

NASA's Ames Research Center began origin-of-life research in 1964, creating "building blocks" of life and charting many steps in the chemical evolution of life. In 1965, launchings began of four spacecraft, the Pioneer 6 through 9 series, to circle the Sun and study solar wind and cosmic rays. In 1989, Pioneer 6—still operating—became history's longest-lived spacecraft, continuing to send back data with an 8-watt Watkins-Johnson amplifier, a traveling-wave tube that was designed to last only three-plus years but instead kept on operating for more than 22 years. Other Ames projects included Biosatellites 1, 2, and 3, which flew plants, insects, fertilized eggs, and a space ape known as Ham in orbit and returned them to Earth, testing the effects of weightlessness on living systems.

In contrast to tiny spacecraft traveling immense distances to explore space beyond Earth orbit, the Stanford Linear Accelerator Center applies tremendous energies to pry open the secrets of tiny particles inside the atom. SLAC was founded in 1962 and in 1966 began research at its two-mile-long electron "gun" in the foothills west of Menlo Park. Large klystron tubes initially speeded the electron beams to energies of 20 billion volts by the time they struck research targets. By 1968, the first evidence was discovered for quarks, the smaller, more fundamental objects within the proton and neutron that are constituents of the atomic nucleus. Richard Taylor of SLAC and two MIT scientists, Jerome Friedman and Henry Kendall, ultimately shared the 1990 Nobel Prize in physics for their quark work. Stanford University operates SLAC for the U.S. Department of Energy.

Stanford Linear Accelerator

Stanford's medical school, a San Francisco fixture for many decades, moved in 1959 to the new Stanford Medical

Pioneer Satellite

Center, straddling the line between Palo Alto and the university. Although some senior faculty members had bitterly opposed the move, it opened the way for more productive collaboration between faculty members in varied scientific fields. Physicians broke fresh ground with the help of new scientific instruments invented and developed at Stanford—linear accelerators, lasers, computer programs, miniaturized instruments made possible by microelectronics.

As the 1960s unfolded, big news kept emerging from the medical center: the first open-heart surgery in 1960, initial "exports" of Stanford-developed linear accelerators for cancer treatment in late 1962, use of lasers to weld detached retinas (led by clinical faculty members Milton Flocks and Christian Zweng of the Palo Alto Medical Clinic), surgical cures of "blue baby" heart defects by Norman Shumway and colleagues, development by researcher Judith Pool of a much superior technique for extracting the blood fraction needed to prevent bleeding in hemophiliacs, installation of the medical school's first computing facility, and, on January 6, 1969, the first heart transplant in an adult patient in the United States, performed by Shumway, Edward Stinson, Eugene Dong, and colleagues.

Palo Alto and Stanford, partners since 1921 in operating a community hospital, went their separate ways in mid-1968 when the university bought out the city's share of their joint hospital. Though now at an end, the city's willingness to shoulder the rare municipal burden of owning a hospital had helped to create a high-ranked modern medical community.

Meanwhile, the 1960s had become the first great era of computers—primarily large computers built to run on IBM software, their operation much enhanced by the disk drives being improved constantly at the San Jose laboratory.

On the industrial front, development of semiconductors was surging. After camping in Palo Alto for a time, Fairchild Semiconductor had made its permanent home in Mountain View. This marked the start of a movement to the south that at length shifted most semiconductor production to Sunnyvale, Santa Clara, and San Jose. That trend was accompanied by a lessening of Stanford University's influence in that aspect of microelectronics, at least for a time. On the whole, output gained momentum, not only in semiconductors but also in ancillary out-sourcing activities, such as printed circuits and crystal growing, and in products for the armed forces: microwave tubes, avionics, and advanced radars.

By 1966 the Midpeninsula was widely recognized as America's largest microelectronics concentration. Two years later, Ampex, which had plunged into consumer products, began to see storm clouds on the horizon.

High - voltage show at Stanford's Ryan Lab

1966

Indira Gandhi is the prime minister of India.

National Organization for women (NOW) is founded.

Assassination of South African prime minister Hendrik Verwoerd.

1967

First successful human heart transplant surgery.

1968

Soviet troops enter Prague and end "Prague Spring" where Czechoslovaks were trying to initiate reforms.

Civil rights leader Martin Luther King is assassinated.

U.S. senator Robert F. Kennedy is assassinated.

1969
Apollo 11 lands on the Moon with U.S. astronauts Neil Armstrong and Edwin Aldrin.

The world's first supersonic passenger aircraft, the Concorde, is created.

1970
Northeastern Africa and southern Sahara experience severe droughts.

Invention of the silicon chip in the U.S. marks a revolution in the electronics industry.

First cases appear of AIDS (Acquired Immune Deficiency Syndrome).

Chapter 11: An Era of Discovery—Moon, Microprocessors, and Gene Manipulation

"That's one small step for a man, one giant leap for mankind," said astronaut Neil Armstrong as he set foot on the Moon. This great U.S. achievement in 1969—thanks in considerable measure to theoretical work, flight simulation, and other NASA/Ames research—demonstrated America's recovery of the aerospace initiative. As the '70s unfolded, NASA/Ames guided the second and third Pioneer series explorations of the outer reaches of the solar system.

Early microprocessor

Meanwhile, the art of packing more and more circuitry onto a fingernail-size silicon chip steadily grew more amazing. When Robert Noyce and Gordon Moore founded Intel Corporation in 1968 (and Arthur Rock raised $5 million in start-up capital for them in 30 minutes on the telephone), they decided to focus on a little-contested part of the market: memory. In 1969 they were producing an 1101 256-bit static RAM (random access memory) for 21 cents per bit. By 1993, that price had been reduced to $.0000029 per bit in an 8-megabit flash chip—just one of Intel's many successes. The phenomenon of ever denser circuits at ever dwindling cost gained expression as "Moore's Law:" memory capacity will double every year, and cost will drop by 20 to 30%.

In 1971, Marcian (Ted) Hoff, still fresh from postgraduate work at Stanford, conceived the microprocessor at Intel, and a talented Italian-born physicist, Federico Faggin, carried through with its development. Hoff's four-chip set, centered around one general-purpose logic device that would access its application instructions from semiconductor memory, replaced 12 custom chips in a programmable calculator—and could be adapted by programs to perform in many different applications. It packed as much computing power as the first electronic computer, the ENIAC, which filled a warehouse when it was built in 1946.

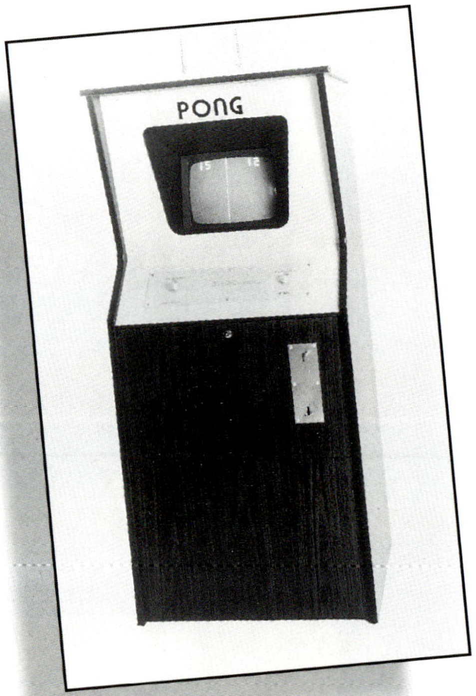

Pong!

Xerox Corporation opened its Palo Alto Research Center in 1970. In ensuing years, PARC scientists developed a dozen groundbreaking computer technologies, some of them growing out of Douglas Englebart's original ideas at Stanford Research Institute. These included portable computing, the laser printer, the first easy-to-use word processing program, and desktop publishing's Postscript language. Other companies—notably Hewlett-Packard, Apple Computer, and Adobe Systems—later exploited most of these innovations.

Semiconductor companies and production had zoomed so much that in 1971 Don Hoefler, editor of *Microelectronics News,* coined the name "Silicon Valley" as shorthand for the whole nexus of wondrous electronics products, instant millionaires, and brand-new industries. Hoefler also traced the history of semiconductor industry

Ted Hoff

spinouts, pegging Fairchild as the most significant and adding, "Fairchild itself has spawned many firms, in instruments and production equipment as well as semiconductors."

More happenings made 1971 a milestone year. Stanford University and Stanford Research Institute cut their ties, the latter becoming independent as SRI International. Gene Amdahl, principal architect in Menlo Park of IBM's highly successful 360 mainframe series, left IBM to develop "plug-compatible manufacturing" at his own company. Also in 1971, Steve Wozniak went to work for Hewlett-Packard as a programmer. After Nolan Bushnell founded Atari in 1972 and began the computer games industry with a game called Pong, Wozniak's younger friend, Steve Jobs, joined Atari.

Although Pong thrived, consumer electronics—epitomized by the digital watch and the basic pocket calculator—enjoyed only a brief heyday in the United States before being crushed by Japanese competition, an event coinciding with the 1974-75 recession. Ampex was especially hard hit.

Biotechnology made one of its first big splashes in 1973 when Stanley N. Cohen of the Stanford medical school faculty and Herbert W. Boyer of the UC San Francisco medical school first demonstrated gene splicing. Patents on gene cloning and gene splicing became the two universities' big earners, with Genentech of South San Francisco a major developer.

Hewlett-Packard introduced the first programmable pocket calculator in 1974, co-opting the place of engineers' slide rules and starting HP in the computer business. In the same year, Siple Station in Antarctica was founded to study upper atmosphere physics in experiments headed by Robert Helliwell, Stanford electrical engineering professor.

At Stanford University, the Center for Integrated Systems took shape in 1974 to coordinate the combined forces of business, government, and higher education in the technology race. One of its codirectors was John Linvill, EE professor and inventor of telesensory processes such as the one enabling his blind daughter to read rapidly—and, in time, to earn a doctorate.

Kenneth Arrow, who had taught at Stanford from 1949 to 1968, and who later returned, was named co-winner of the 1972 Nobel Prize for economics for his contributions to welfare economics and general economic equilibrium theory. Paul J. Flory of Stanford received the 1974 Nobel Prize for chemistry for his investigations of synthetic and natural polymers, the macromolecules developed most notably in nylon and synthetic rubber.

Intel founders: Andy Grove, Bob Noyce, Gordon Moore

1972

Arab terrorists of "Black September" organization kill Israeli athletes, disrupting the Munich Olympics.

Watergate scandal breaks out when U.S. Republican presidential aides bug Democratic headquarters.

1973

Arab and Israeli 'Yom-Kippur' War.

Oil crisis in the U.S. and Europe.

U.S. Supreme Court rules 7-2 in Roe v. Wade granting women the legal option to abortion during the first trimester of pregnancy.

1974

President Richard Nixon resigns.

James G. Treybig, Tandem CEO (standing), and Thomas J. Perkins, board chairman, are longtime associates

It wasn't until the late 1960s that major corporations first began using computers to handle their business operations. Back then, few could have predicted what a fundamental part of American business computer technology would become. As the volume of transactions required by banks, manufacturers, airlines, railroads, stock exchanges, and other industries steadily grew, so did the demand for larger systems to handle the rapid stream of deposits, withdrawals, inventory changes, reservations, and stock transfers.

By the early 1970s, online transaction processing, or OLTP, had become an essential business tool. The company that pioneered that technology was Tandem Computers Incorporated.

Founded in 1974 by a group headed by James G. Treybig, current president and CEO, Tandem produced the world's first fault-tolerant OLTP computer system. Today, the company is one of the world's leading suppliers of continuously available, online computer systems.

A system that is "fault-tolerant" is one that employs dual main processors and special operating software that keep the system operating even if any single point of failure should occur. Treybig pioneered the first fault-tolerant system, Tandem's NonStop system.

A native of Houston, Texas, Treybig studied engineering at Rice University and earned his MBA at Stanford University. After graduating from Stanford, he went to work for Tom Perkins at Hewlett-Packard.

Like many young, ambitious engineers in Silicon Valley, Treybig's dream was to establish his own company. To gain experience in the financial world, he eventually left HP to join his former boss at the venture capital firm of Kleiner-Perkins (now Kleiner, Perkins, Caulfield & Byers).

Perkins and his partner, Eugene Kleiner, were unique among venture capitalists of the day. Both were engineers with hands-on experience at their own start-up high-tech companies. Perkins had cofounded University Labs, which later merged with Spectra-Physics, and Kleiner was one of the so-called "traitorous eight" who founded Fairchild Semiconductor.

Treybig eventually approached Perkins and Kleiner with his idea for a high-tech start-up. His innovative plan involved producing fail-safe, modular computer systems that offered distributed processing without the need to change hardware or software. Treybig's system would also compete in price with the industry giants such as IBM.

With encouragement from Perkins and Kleiner, Treybig started looking around the Valley for the technical expertise he would need for his as-yet-unformed company. He began by approaching former colleagues from his HP days, speaking first with Jim Katzman, who had helped design the HP 3000 before leaving HP to take a position at Amdahl. He also approached Mike Green, who had designed the industry's first time-sharing system, also at HP. Both were excited by the technical and professional challenges of a start-up environment.

In mid-1974, Perkins put up $50,000 to recruit Green and Katzman for Treybig's project. Jack Loustaunou of Kleiner-Perkins joined the group to provide the financial expertise. With four months' lead time—a rare luxury for start-ups—the five men worked out a detailed development plan for the new company.

Treybig later recalled in a 1981 interview for *Inc.* magazine, "We worked out all aspects in advance—people, finance, manufacturing, everything. We could afford to because we weren't starving to death. One

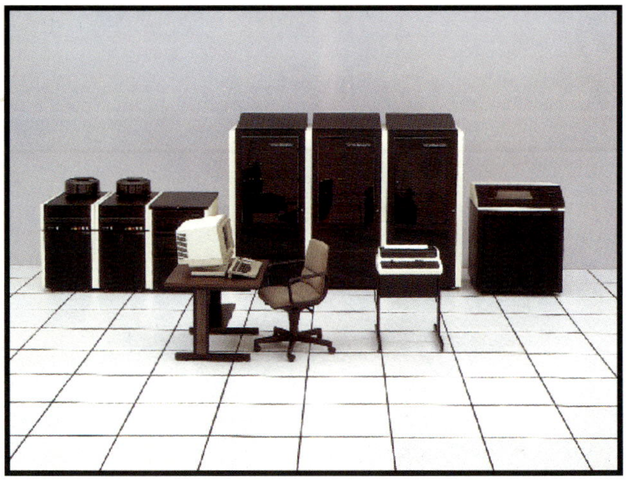

Tandem produced the first fault-tolerant OLTP computer system. Pictured is an early NonStop computer system

Integrity S4000 Server, with ServerNet architecture providing a high-performance interconnect between processors and I/O devices

reason we have been able to grow so fast and not have problems was that we thought through most of the potential problems before we started."

The group began developing their business plan in late June of 1974 and finished in mid-November. Katzman remembers putting in regular workdays at Amdahl, and then going straight to work on the plan each evening. The plan included details of system design and architecture, financing, and teamwork, as well as the people-oriented atmosphere that was such an important part of Treybig's vision.

Convinced by the model business plan and the top-flight management team, and despite an uncertain economy, Kleiner and Perkins invested an additional $1 million in the enterprise. The company was launched with venture capital, in a recession, and without a name.

The group kept a growing list of possible names for the company, rotating a new name to the top every day. Among the early contenders were Dandi Data (which Perkins thought would get attention), Redundant Computers (until future employee Dave Mackie pointed out that "redundant" could mean "unnecessary"), and Multi Data (at the top of the list the day funding was secured). On the day the call came from the California Securities Commission for a name to put on the incorporation papers, the name at the top of the list was one that had been suggested by Green: Tandem.

On May 28, 1976, Tandem shipped its first NonStop processors to Citicorp to run their phone directory.

Tandem began as a single-system provider without much of a software offering. But within a few years, the company was providing both high- and low-end systems with a full complement of software, particularly in the networking area. During its first 10 years, Tandem successfully anticipated the changing needs of its market and quickly joined the ranks of the *Fortune 500*. The company entered the 1990s with more than 5,000 employees and $1.6 billion in revenues.

Today, Tandem computers are widely used in banking, telecommunications, retail, manufacturing, and other industries around the world. More than 30 of the world's largest stock and futures exchanges and over 60 securities firms run on Tandem systems. More than 300 banks utilize Tandem technology. Tandem systems are in use in more than half of the nation's largest electronic funds transfer networks.

Telecommunications has become a major source of business for Tandem. Worldwide, more than 70 telecommunications companies use Tandem systems for such applications as network management, information gateways, and service order entries.

Tandem systems run ATMs, point-of-sale networks, and other networks where hundreds of business transactions must be processed each second and recorded instantly.

Large retailers use Tandem systems to approve credit requests, ensure adequate merchandise distribution, and retrieve store sales data electronically.

Hundreds of firms in production-intensive industries, such as automobiles, aerospace, electronics, pharmaceuticals, and food manufacture, use Tandem computers to integrate their operations. Applications in these industries include shop-floor control, work-in-process tracking, collection and analysis of quality-control data, and inventory management.

Headquartered in Cupertino, California, in the heart of Silicon Valley, Tandem maintains nearly 70 sales offices in the United States, with subsidiaries operating in Europe, Asia, Australia, and South America. The company's manufacturing plants are located in Fremont, California, and Stirling, Scotland. Tandem employs more than 8,500 people worldwide.

Jimmy Treybig is Tandem's co-founder, president and chief executive officer

AMD is the fourth-largest U.S.-based merchant supplier of integrated circuits

Advanced Micro Devices stands today as the fourth-largest U.S-based merchant manufacturer of integrated circuits, with more than $2 billion in annual sales. Headed since its inception by W.J. (Jerry) Sanders III, the company is a technology leader, with innovative products and world-class manufacturing capacity. AMD ranks either first or second in market share in each of its core businesses: microprocessors, nonvolatile memories, programmable logic devices, and circuits for communications and networking applications.

To gain a place among America's semiconductor giants, AMD had to rise above humble beginnings and endure epic struggles. Sanders remembers an *Innovation* magazine article evaluating 1969 semiconductor start-ups that said AMD faced "the most uncertainty." To Sanders, that felt like being named "least likely to succeed." Today AMD is established beyond any uncertainty, and *Innovation* magazine is defunct.

Like many of Silicon Valley's companies, AMD was founded by former Fairchild Semiconductor employees. In May 1969, eight ex-Fairchild workers formed AMD, with Sanders at the lead. An electrical engineer from the University of Illinois, Sanders had starred at Fairchild by melding his grasp of technology with a mastery of marketing.

The founding eight — Jack Gifford, Sven Simonsen, John Carey, Jim Giles, Ed Turney, Larry Stenger, Frank Botte, and Sanders — put up $50,000 to start the company. It took them a year to overcome a stock market dip and doubtful venture capitalists and raise $1,505,000.

AMD started as a second-source company offering standard products. At its inception, the company recognized that its success depended upon making an important contribution to the success of its customers. AMD chose to provide value by offering superior products at the same cost as its competitors and standard products at a lower cost.

AMD's first revenue came in 1970 from a 4-bit shift register. The next year the company entered the memory market with a 64-bit RAM. In 1972, AMD went public, opened an assembly plant in Penang, Malaysia, and built rapidly near its Sunnyvale headquarters. Recession struck in 1974, but AMD weathered it, even opening its third fab.

During a brief recession in 1981, Sanders vowed that AMD would continue R&D investment, hard times or no. By 1984, business was booming. Then in the third quarter, the bottom suddenly dropped out of the market. By 1985, a worldwide industry recession led to the dumping of DRAM (dynamic random access memory) and EPROM (electrically programmable read only memory) products, and tremendous trade friction between the United States and Japan. The entire industry was rocked, but AMD was especially hard-hit because it had been busily investing in new manufacturing capacity and slow to convert to a new manufacturing technology, which later became the industry standard.

The crisis triggered a transformation that ultimately changed a second-source company into an innovator of high-performance proprietary products. In transforming itself, AMD first used a familiar strategy. Despite the bad economy, it risked investing heavily in R&D and new manufacturing facilities. In 1987 the company invested an initial $200 million in the Submicron Development Center, a cutting-edge wafer manufacturing facility that enabled the company to develop advanced, submicron process technology and eventually become a technology leader.

The transformation also entailed beefing up the company. A 1987 merger with Monolithic Memories gave AMD a leadership product (programmable logic devices) and strengthened the balance sheet. As it progressed, the transformation involved redefining the company's mission, closing 10 aging fabs, and focusing on markets where the company could be a leader, thus discontinuing hundreds of products.

The transformation worked. By 1991 AMD's new focus had enabled the company to build an enhanced 386 microprocessor family that filled market gaps left by the dominant microprocessor supplier, Intel Corporation, and restored competition to the PC market.

AMD has several state-of-the-art test and assembly facilities in Asia

In late 1995, AMD will begin volume production at Fab 25, a $1.2 billion "megafab" that is among the most advanced wafer fabrication facilities in the world. AMD will also introduce the AMD-K5™ device, the company's first microprocessor built on its proprietary, superscalar RISC-based architecture. The AMD-K5 will complete AMD's transformation from an alternate supplier of standard products to a technology leader and innovator.

As AMD's first completely independently engineered microprocessor, the AMD-K5 will also mark the final conclusion of a historic eight-year legal struggle with Intel that officially ended in early 1995.

Back in 1976, AMD and Intel signed a copyright license agreement. In the early 1980s, IBM introduced its first PC, decided to pursue an open architecture to assure that the market would grow faster, and selected Intel's X86 microprocessor architecture, making it the industry standard. IBM wanted a second source for its X86 products, so in 1982 AMD signed an agreement to be a second source for Intel's microprocessors.

With the success of IBM — and of countless "IBM clone" suppliers — the market exploded. Then in 1985, Intel introduced the 386 microprocessor, and disagreements began. In 1987, AMD attempted to compel arbitration over disputes concerning the 1982 agreement, a process the company expected would take six weeks. Instead, the arbitration spawned new lawsuits, including cases on the 287 microcode, the X86 nomenclature, and the 386 and 486 microprocessors. Each side won some and lost some as cases went into appeals, decisions were reversed, and retrials ensued. The fight cost AMD $100 million in legal bills. It finally ended in a settlement, within two weeks after AMD won a California Supreme Court appeal on the original arbitration dispute. Nine months earlier, a federal court jury had held for AMD in the 287 microcode case.

Under terms of the settlement, Intel paid $18 million owed to AMD for breach of contract, AMD paid Intel $58 million for a previous loss in a module of the 486 case, AMD gained a perpetual license to the microcode in the 386 and 486 microprocessors, and a new patent cross-licensing agreement was negotiated.

Throughout AMD's struggles and successes, a few key philosophies have remained consistent. An early quote — "People first; products and profits will follow" — sums up AMD's commitment to people as the only sustainable source of competitive advantage. This principle sometimes wears spangles. One year Sanders handed out gold coins as payments under AMD's long-standing profit-sharing program. The company also has a tradition of throwing lavish parties for its employees. Because of the company's

Rod Stewart sang in 1994 at a 25th anniversary party for AMD employees and their families

commitment to its people, all three editions of *The 100 Best Companies to Work for in America* have honored AMD.

Being a good corporate citizen and neighbor is another tenet. AMD has been a leader in environmental health and safety programs, charitable contributions, involvement in the community, and support of education. The company has a strong employee volunteerism program.

Sanders is a leader intensely loyal to his workers and customers. AMD considers itself customer-driven and supports open standards of product architecture and process.

"Our only business," Sanders says, "is providing solutions in silicon that enable our customers to gain a competitive edge in the marketplace. We do this by offering differentiated products that lower the cost, improve the performance and reduce the time to market for our customers' products. We believe in competition as the principal driving force for progress and productivity — but we don't compete with our customers! Their success is our success."

In 1969 AMD President Richard Previte (left) joined the eight founders, including CEO Jerry Sanders (right)

ROLM founders, from left, Gene Richeson, Robert Maxfield, M. Kenneth Oshman, and Walter Lowenstern

The four former Texans who founded ROLM in 1969 didn't know they were about to pioneer a new era of private telecommunications in the United States. They just wanted to have a company of their own. It turned out to be a pace-setting success, and now is part of Siemens, world leader in the private communications market.

The founders–Gene Richeson, Kenneth Oshman, Walter Lowenstern Jr. and Robert Maxfield–all were electrical engineering graduates of Rice University in Houston who had gone on to advanced studies at Stanford University and employment in Silicon Valley in the '60s. "ROLM" came from the first initials of their surnames.

Lowenstern spurred them to action after he quit his job at Sylvania's Electronic Defense Laboratory in Mountain View, California, because his boss insisted he drop his interest in a business opportunity Sylvania had turned down.

Richeson and Oshman also were working for Sylvania, Maxfield for IBM. It was Richeson who had the idea for a first product–a ruggedized computer for military uses. Maxfield was recruited by the other three because he knew something about computers. They started business in an abandoned prune drying shed, quickly developed a prototype general-purpose digital computer, and shipped their first order in March 1970. ROLM was profitable from the start.

ROLM settled in Santa Clara. Oshman presided, Maxfield headed engineering, Lowenstern worked with administration and personnel, and Richeson dealt with sales.

The Mil-Spec computers did well. In a few years the company began looking for a way to diversify by applying their computer expertise to other products. After investigating numerous opportunities, they decided to combine a computer with a telephone switchboard–a PBX. Industry sources liked the idea of using digital computer switching technology in PBXs, but judged it years away from economic feasibility. ROLM leaders saw it as closer, and made plans to get a jump on the market.

So in 1975 the company leaped into the new arena. It was risky, because AT&T was talking of challenging the Carter administration decision to open competition in the telephone equipment marketplace.

ROLM's new product, the CBX–a computer-controlled telephone system–was designed to cut costs and increase productivity. It automatically put long-distance calls through by the cheapest route, and, if the line was busy, the computer would try the call again and ring the caller. Its more than 80 features turned out to be very popular. Early distribution was solely through independent telephone companies and independent interconnect distributors. ROLM made a policy of taking good care of its distributors.

New products came out in a steady stream. In 1979, ROLM introduced the first microprocessor-controlled telephone, the ETS100, which shipped in large quantities. In 1982 the company introduced PhoneMail, followed the next year by Cypress and a family of telephones keyed to a goal of user friendliness. By then an objective of creating a complete business communications system had taken shape.

ROLM was considered one of Silicon Valley's hottest companies in 1984 when the news broke of a proposed merger with International Business Machines Corporation. Analysts saw IBM/ROLM as a powerful potential competitor of AT&T. After shareholders approved the merger, ROLM Corporation continued to operate as a wholly owned subsidiary of IBM, and Oshman stayed for about a year as president.

In Silicon Valley, ROLM was known for its informal style and lush recreational facilities, and some observers foresaw a culture clash with more buttoned-up IBM.

IBM subsequently made ROLM a division and later integrated it into IBM's Communication

ROLMphone 600 series telephones with snap-in modules offer a variety of features and functions

No tools are required to adapt a ROLMphone 600 to new functionality

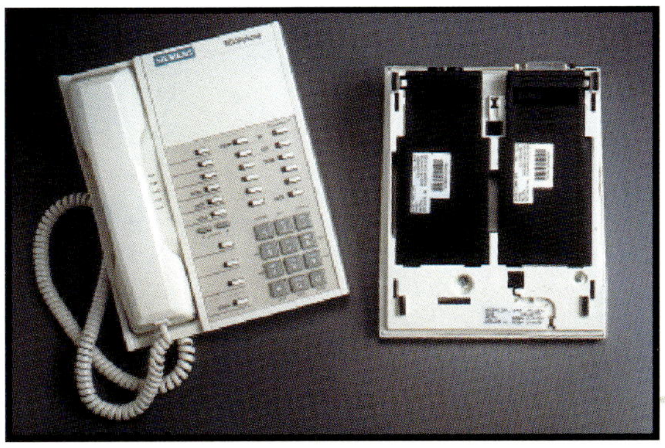

Systems line of business.

During the mid-1980s, Siemens stepped up its U.S. activities. The company, founded in Germany in 1847, had always had telecommunications as a central role. Long before AT&T incorporated, Siemens designed and installed the first commercial telegraph system and a 7,000-mile telegraph link between London and Calcutta. In 1874, Siemens laid the first transatlantic cable between America and Europe. In 1986, Siemens acquired Tel Plus, then the largest independent U.S. interconnect.

Thus the stage was set by 1988 for Siemens to begin its buyout of ROLM. First it acquired IBM's ROLM development and manufacturing operations in Santa Clara and Austin, Texas. These were merged with telecommunication development operations of Siemens Information Systems (SIS) in Boca Raton, Florida, and manufacturing operations in Cherry Hill, New Jersey. Tel Plus continued under SIS. Siemens and IBM also established a joint marketing and services partnership for ROLM products in the United States.

In May 1992, Siemens completed its acquisition of ROLM, making the Santa Clara company the U.S. business unit of Siemens Private Communications Systems. Later that year Siemens consolidated all of its U.S. private communication units into a single company now called Siemens Rolm Communications Inc.

Peter Pribilla, former president and chief executive officer of Siemens Rolm Communications, remarked that the "name change demonstrates Siemens' commitment to customers in the North American market and more accurately reflects our presence in the global marketplace ... " Day-to-day operations and the strategic business direction would not be affected, he said.

Siemens AG has worldwide sales of approximately $55 billion a year. Siemens Private Communication Systems Group, of which Siemens Rolm is part, has more than 450,000 customers and 900,000 systems installed worldwide and annual sales of $4.5 billion.

The Santa Clara-based company has almost 6,000 employees. Karl Geng is its president and CEO. In addition to its manufacturing facilities in three cities, it has three research and development centers. Siemens as a whole spends $20 million plus each working day on R&D. Siemens Rolm has nearly 150 sales and services locations serving more than 30,000 customers in the U.S. and Canada. Through Siemens, it has worldwide presence in 132 countries.

Private communication systems from Siemens Rolm can serve companies with as few as 30 lines at a single location, or multinational organizations needing more than 20,000 lines at one or many sites.

Today's Siemens Rolm digital switching products include the 9751 CBX, for up to 20,000 or more lines, and the 9200 CBX for 30 to 80 lines, plus a selection of full-featured digital telephones.

Applications include PhoneMail voice processing products, ISDN and private networking, automatic call distribution, interactive voice response units, and telemanagement products. CallBridge for Desktops, another application, connects a worker's PC and telephone, enabling dialing, logging calls and accessing voice mail, faxes, E-mail, and the phone directory all through one point-and-click screen.

Siemens Rolm is committed to industry standards. The reason is to enable customers with private systems to operate in a multivendor communications environment, utilizing open PBX architecture, standardized networking protocols, ISDN (integrated services digital network) framework and application programming interface (ADI).

The company's proud record of innovation and quality attests that Siemens Rolm will remain in the vanguard of future Silicon Valley progress.

Siemens Rolm's ComManager PRO brings together the power of the PC and the telephone for point and click dialing

Etec Systems, Inc.

Etec Systems, Inc., of Hayward, California, began its corporate life in 1970 as a manufacturer of scanning electron microscopes. In 1975, using technologies licensed from AT&T and its own expertise with electron beam columns, Etec developed MEBES—the first commercially available, production-worthy, electron-beam mask-writing lithography system.

Mask writing, also called pattern generation, is the first critical step in the production of semiconductor devices. A mask is created to be used like a photographic negative to transfer a chip design onto a silicon wafer. The pattern is transferred to the mask in portions that must align, or overlay, nearly perfectly.

Etec's first MEBES system embodied new technology with the use of electron-beam writing and also provided superior overlay capabilities and higher throughput than existing commercial systems. These capabilities led to the next generation of chip designs, and MEBES allowed the devices to actually be produced.

Fairchild Semiconductor purchased MEBES serial number 1 in 1976 and harnessed this breakthrough in new mask technologies. Fairchild employees later founded or led many companies that became significant in the history of Silicon Valley, including National Semiconductor, Intel Corporation, and Advanced Micro Devices. MEBES serial number 10 went to Micromask, the first maskmaking company to purchase a commercial electron-beam maskmaking system.

Within five years MEBES systems had become the standard for maskmaking in the integrated circuit industry. In 1979 the company was acquired by Perkin-Elmer, becoming its Electron Beam Technology Division. In 1990, however, Perkin-Elmer exited the semiconductor equipment industry. The division became the company as it is known today, Etec Systems, Inc. It is supported by a consortium comprising DuPont, Northrop Grumman, IBM, Micron Technology, and Zitel. Chuck Minihan, EBT division general manager from 1980 to 1985, came out of retirement to forge the consortium and run the new company.

Etec's first generation MEBES®, or Manufacturing Electron Beam Exposure System, 1977

Meanwhile, in Beaverton, Oregon, ATEQ Corporation had been founded in 1983 by C. Neil Berglund and Barry Cox. Berglund, a veteran of Bell Laboratories and Intel Corporation, had a clear idea how to use lasers in a semiconductor processing machine. Within two years, ATEQ had a laser-based product up and running.

ATEQ, with its CORE (Custom Optical Reticle Engraver) systems, became the leading supplier of laser-based lithography systems for maskmaking and direct-write applications, and was Etec's prime competitor.

In November 1991 Etec completed a merger with ATEQ, ending their marketplace rivalry. Stephen E. Cooper, who succeeded Minihan as president and CEO in 1993, managed to bring the two divisions into harmony while maintaining separate operations at Hayward and Beaverton. Today, Etec's electron- and laser-beam lithography systems command over 70% market share in the industry. The company has an installed base of 148 advanced commercial pattern-generation systems of an estimated 220 systems worldwide outside the former Eastern Bloc countries.

As Etec marked its 25th anniversary, two of the six founders, Dave Colby and George Bertuccelli, were still employees. At Beaverton, Paul Warkentin, one of ATEQ's first hires, is now a vice president. Etec has international offices in Europe, Japan, and Korea.

Today, the industry is again poised for new growth as the technologies emerge that will allow the creation of the "next generation" of smaller semiconductor devices. Maskmaking will again play a key role, as will the newest electron-beam and laser-beam pattern generation systems from Etec Systems, Inc.

Etec is headquartered in Hayward, California, with laser operations in Beaverton, Oregon

Northern Telecom (Nortel) has grown from its beginnings in 1895 as a small manufacturer of telephones in Montréal to its present status as a leading global provider in the design, building, and integration of information, entertainment, and communications networks.

Nortel scored a coup in 1976 when it introduced digital technology to the telecommunications industry. Today it has the largest installed base of fully digital switching systems in the world.

When Nortel established its first Silicon Valley facility in Mountain View in 1974, the manufacturing operation had only 20 employees. They produced an electronic small-business communications system, and had virtually none of the growing PBX (private branch exchange) market.

Since that time, Nortel's Meridian 1 PBX system and its predecessor, the SL-1, have emerged as the world's leading business communication systems, with over 80,000 systems installed in more than 90 countries worldwide.

In 1979, manufacturing operations, along with 600 employees, were moved from Mountain View to the current location in Santa Clara. Due to rapid increase in product demand, the Santa Clara plant was expanded in 1981 and again in 1984.

Nortel also established its research and development presence in Silicon Valley by opening a laboratory in Palo Alto in 1975. In 1980, the lab and its 450 employees moved to a new 162,000 square-foot facility in Mountain View.

Nortel maintained those two facilities in Silicon Valley until it integrated the Meridian 1 R & D organization with the manufacturing operations in an expanded and remodeled campus in Santa Clara in 1995. This move consolidated Nortel's world headquarters for PBX development and manufacturing in one location. About 1,400 people are employed there at the 420,000 square-foot facilities. Other Nortel PBX labs and manufacturing sites around the globe are linked closely to the Santa Clara operations.

Nortel employees enthusiastically support the local community with volunteer programs including mentoring middle school children in math, holding shadowing days to encourage students to stay in school, and gathering contributions for area food banks. The company provides financial support for local assistance agencies, the arts, and public libraries.

In observance of its centennial anniversary in 1995, the corporation adopted its new Nortel logo, with the "O" stylized as a "globemark" to symbolize its global reach. The new signature "Nortel" does not sound strange to employees and customers-the term has long been a shorthand for the company name.

Headquartered in Mississauga, Ontario, just outside Toronto, Nortel had 1994 revenues of US$8.9 billion, and 57,000 employees worldwide. Despite its Canadian base and background, the company has a major presence in the United States where it has extensive facilities and employs about 22,000 people.

1980's vintage robotics equipment used to assemble printed circuit boards

Gray Cary Ware & Freidenrich was created Jan. 1, 1994, by the merger of Ware & Freidenrich, Silicon Valley's second largest law firm, and Gray Cary Ames & Frye, San Diego's largest. Based in California's two most important areas for emerging technology and biotechnology companies, the combined firm managed 29 public offerings in its first 18 months and advised numerous clients on mergers and acquisitions.

Now one of California's leading professional legal corporations with 280 attorneys in six offices, Gray Cary is a full-service commercial law firm providing corporate, business, litigation, intellectual property, finance, real estate, employment, tax, and estate planning services.

The Palo Alto side of the new team originated in 1969, when Leo Ware and John Freidenrich set up their firm. Their practice gravitated to business and high technology and grew with the region that became known as "Silicon Valley." From a core client base of high technology start-ups, the firm expanded to represent a wide range of successful public and private companies located primarily in Northern California and doing business globally.

By the time of the merger, founders Ware and Freidenrich both had retired from active law practice, and the firm numbered about 100 attorneys. Ware busied himself rendering arbitration and mediation services on behalf of the American Arbitration Association, as well as government units, other organizations, and individuals. Freidenrich became the general partner in a prestigious Silicon Valley venture capital group and an active volunteer in charity work. He currently serves as chairman of the Stanford University Board of Trustees.

Gray Cary Ames & Frye started in 1927, and took its pre-merger name in 1934. It , too, grew with its region as San Diego sprouted industries in the electronics, telecommunications, biotechnology, biomedicine, health care, hospitality, manufacturing, media, construction, and real estate fields. Gray Cary also has built a substantial Mexican business practice.

Both firms had proud records of pro bono (for the public good) service, and the merged firm is continuing that tradition. In 1995, it received San Diego Pro Bono Law Firm of the Year honors for the third consecutive year. Recently, the firm was recognized as Southern California Pro Bono Law Firm of the Year.

When the merger was announced, regional legal newspapers noted Gray Cary's depth in trial lawyers and Ware's securities experience and venture capital contacts. Gray Cary was said to seek a higher profile among San Diego's high-tech entrepreneurs, and Ware more trial work for its existing client base including *Fortune* 500 companies.

John Freidenrich, law firm co-founder and venture capitalist

Leo Ware, co-founder, Ware & Freidenrich

Gray Cary Ware & Freidenrich now has offices in Palo Alto, San Jose, San Diego, La Jolla, and El Centro, with affiliate offices in Tijuana and Mexico City. In November 1994, the firm opened a new office in the Golden Triangle—the heart of San Diego's technology cluster. Paul Kreutz, a senior corporate attorney with extensive experience advising emerging companies, relocated from Palo Alto to lead the Golden Triangle office.

The firm is headed by two cochairmen, Don G. Rushing in San Diego and Gregory M. Gallo in Palo Alto. (Gallo was recently named by *California Law Business* as one of Silicon Valley's "Top 20 Lawyers at the Forefront of Technology.")

In 1994-95 mergers and acquisitions, the firm represented SynOptics Communications in a record merger with Wellfleet Communications, valued at $1.1 billion, to form Bay Networks, Inc. The firm maintains a leading position in both mergers and acquisitions and the public offerings arena.

With over 25 years' experience in Silicon Valley serving start-ups to *Fortune* 500 companies, and with special expertise counseling emerging companies, Gray Cary Ware & Freidenrich will continue to be a major force in 21st century high-technology law

Greg Gallo, co-chair, Gray Cary Ware & Freidenrich

Vision. The ability to consistently anticipate and bring forth solutions to ever-changing needs. That is the key to the staying power of Knight-Ridder Information, Inc., and Dialog, the world's premier electronic information system. Born at the dawn of the Information Age, Knight-Ridder Information remains the world leader in electronic information services.

In 1960—when Roger Summit, then a doctoral candidate in management science at Stanford University, took a summer job working in the information processing department of Lockheed Missiles and Space Company—the online information industry did not exist. Summit stayed on at Lockheed, and in 1963, he and his group began to design the structure that became the foundation for today's online retrieval technology. In 1968, Lockheed won a contract from NASA to provide an interactive online retrieval system for aerospace research. Contracts with other government agencies, such as the U.S. Department of Education, followed.

Dialog Information Services became a commercial entity in 1972, headquartered in Palo Alto, California. By 1981, Dialog offered more than 150 databases and that year became a wholly owned subsidiary of Lockheed Corporation.

Throughout the 1980s, founder Summit continued to lead the company as its president, consistently expanding the breadth and quality of its services. In 1988, to provide further product and technological opportunities, Dialog was purchased by Knight-Ridder, Inc., an international information and communications company. In 1993, Data-Star, Europe's leading online service, became part of the company's global information service.

Today, over 200,000 customers in almost 150 countries use the 600-plus Dialog and Data Star databases, providing business, news, scientific, and technical information. Knight-Ridder Information also offers electronic mail and electronic delivery of online search results, and both Macintosh and IBM-compatible personal computer communications software and CD-ROM databases. Knight-Ridder Information also offers a comprehensive, worldwide document delivery service. Easy-to-use Windows-based applications for a variety of platforms, including the Internet, are under development.

In 1995, Dialog changed its name to Knight-Ridder Information, Inc., and moved its headquarters to Mountain View, California. The massive computer center remains a few miles away in Palo Alto. With its creative diligence in meeting the needs of the market, this "granddaddy" of electronic information remains at the industry's forefront with the world's largest and most comprehensive databank.

Roger Summit, founder of Dialog (now Knight-Ridder Information), in the computer room in 1984

Bill Hewlett holding the HP-35 handheld scientific calculator—first introduced in 1972

1975
Japanese company JVC creates VHS (Video Home System).

1976
African schoolchildren uprisings in Soweto, South Africa.

Zhou Enlai's and Mao Zedong's deaths put an end to the "Gang of Four".

Earthquake in Tang Shan China kills 240,000.

1977
Astronauts observe rings around planet Uranus.

1978
Egypt and Israel sign Camp David treaty.

World 's first "test tube" baby born in U.K.

1979
Margaret Thatcher is the first female prime minister of England.

First Apple I

Chapter 12: Personal Computer Bursts Hobby Bonds

If you wanted an inexpensive microcomputer in 1975, you had one choice: Spend $498 on an Altair 8800 hobby kit, with Intel's third microprocessor, the 8080, at its heart. Once built, there was little you could do with it; still, the innovation excited techies. In March 1975, they formed the Homebrew Computer Club in Menlo Park, and soon drew turnouts so large they had to get permission to use SLAC's auditorium.

Steve Wozniak was a founding Homebrewer. When he saw the home computers others built, "Woz" felt he could do better. Buying a microprocessor cheap at a computer show, he built a machine around it, and at club meetings showed it and handed out copies of his design. The Apple I was an instant hit. His friend Steve Jobs suggested forming a company, and in 1976 Apple Computer started up in Jobs' Cupertino garage. Jobs, 20, and Wozniak, 25, moonlighted to fill orders until they could no longer meet the demand. Despite their pleas, their respective employers declined to adopt the product.

While Wozniak improved the design, Jobs sought backing. He was put in touch with A.C. (Mike) Markkula, 40, an Intel marketer then planning to retire early. Impressed by the Apple, Markkula persuaded the Steves to do a business plan, arranged financing, invested money of his own and stayed with the new company. In 1977 they introduced the Apple II, featuring a bold innovation, floppy-disk controllers, and Wozniak's simple but elegant design. Fully assembled (as Jobs sensed buyers wanted), it outstripped all projections, creating a PC market and sales topping $100 million by 1980.

On the large computer front, Tandem, a company started by James Treybig in 1974, worked on fault-tolerant computers. Amdahl, meanwhile, shipped its first plug-in compatible product in 1975. But the firm remained under heavy pressure due to underfinancing and IBM's rivalry. Gene Amdahl resigned in 1979; he later associated with Trilogy and Grid Systems. Another Amdahl employee, Lawrence Ellison, joined Robert Miner and Edward Oates in forming Oracle Systems in 1977 to create a relational database management system meeting theoretical specifications published by IBM.

As for semiconductors, equipment vendors who founded the Semiconductor Equipment and Materials Institute in 1970 were having marked success. By 1975, their drive to set standards aimed at reducing waste, inventory and planning reached pay dirt. More than 80% of all new wafers met SEMI standards—a remarkable feat because Silicon Valley was approaching a 1980 census of close to 3,000 manufacturing companies. The manufacturers' group, the Western Electronics Manufacturing Association (WEMA), was renamed the American Electronics Association (AEA) in 1978. Intel

Steven Wozniak

Yamaha DX-7

marketed a microprocessor-based OEM (original equipment manufacturer) system in 1976—the first single-board computer. At National Semiconductor, Charles Sporck had honed manufacturing skills and made DRAMs (dynamic random access memories) a commodity product.

Steven Jobs

Silicon Valley scientists and engineers were puzzled by the emphasis Japanese companies were putting on CMOS (complementary metal oxide silicon) technology, which Fairchild had tried and discarded. Intel made limited use of CMOS in digital watches, but quit making them in 1979. CMOS was slow and drew relatively little power. The Japanese, with shrewd marketing eyes, saw its advantages in portable devices—watches, calculators, cameras, and TVs.

At Stanford University, the process of transferring faculty inventions to commercial firms to develop had taken shape in the Office of Technology Licensing. By 1980, OTL under Niels Reimers had helped professors patent more than 400 inventions, earning Stanford $61 million in royalties. The top money-earner proved to be music Professor John Chowning's FM synthesis. Chowning had discovered in 1967 that at a certain frequency, patterns of vibrations from two oscillators generated harmonic tones like those of musical instruments. Yamaha Corp. bought exclusive use of his 1977 patent, and in 1984 introduced its DX7 synthesizer, a must for rock bands and one of the most popular instruments ever.

NASA/Ames Research Center dedicated the Kuiper Airborne Observatory in 1975—a converted C-141 transport plane equipped with a 36-inch infrared telescope. In 1977, scientists aboard the Kuiper discovered that the planet Uranus possesses equatorial rings, composed of rock and ice. Later discoveries included Venus cloud composition, galactic center phenomena, star formation, and supernova mechanisms. In 1978, the Stanford-NASA Joint Institute for Surface and Microstructural Research formalized a collaboration begun in 1968. University departments of materials science, chemical engineering and electrical engineering were involved.

Three Stanford faculty superstars became Nobel laureates in the 1975-80 period. Burton Richter won the 1976 physics prize for his work at the Linear Accelerator Center in discovering the existence of the psi or J particle. Richter subsequently became SLAC's director. Milton Friedman won the 1976 economics prize for championing laissez-faire economics and, the next year, came to Stanford's Hoover Institution after 30 years at the University of Chicago. Paul Berg won the 1980 chemistry prize for his development of recombinant DNA techniques—work subsequently applied by a number of San Francisco Bay Area biotechnology companies.

1979

Somoza government undergoes civil war in Nicaragua; Sandinistas seize power.

Sony chairman Akio Morita of Japan invents portable stereo (the Walkman).

Philips and Sony develop the compact disc.

Mobile or cellular telephone is invented in Sweden.

U.S. attempt to rescue hostages in Iran fails.

Park Chung Hee, South Korean president, is assassinated.

1980

Guerrilla war; Zimbabwe gains independence.

Beginning of Iran-Iraq war.

Civil war in El Salvador; (1980-92).

U.S. space shuttle launched.

Lawrence J. Ellison has been Oracle's CEO since he co-founded the company in 1977

When Oracle Corporation cofounder, chairman, and CEO Lawrence J. Ellison first landed in Santa Clara in the late 1960s at the age of 21, he quickly realized he wasn't in South Chicago anymore. He found himself smack in the middle of a magical land of silicon chips and circuit boards, where strangely named languages such as "Assembly" and "Cobol" were written, but not spoken. Undaunted, this adopted son of Russian Jewish immigrants applied his brains, courage, and heart–as well his educational background in math and physics–to the task, taught himself programming, and entered the whirlwind world of high technology.

Today, from the towers of "Emerald City" (as Oracle's dazzling complex at the northern edge of Silicon Valley has been dubbed), Ellison reigns as the Wizard of Database Technology. Oracle is the world's leading supplier of information management software, a \$3 billion enterprise with over 17,000 employees in over 90 countries.

The gold-bricked road to Oracle's current stellar position began in 1977 when Ellison hooked up with cofounder Robert N. Miner, whom he had met when they worked at Omex Corporation in Sunnyvale. Both men had experience designing customized software programs for various government agencies, which they parlayed into a contract to build a specialized database for the Central Intelligence Agency (CIA).

With \$1,800 in pooled savings and a vision to create an "enjoyable work environment they hoped would grow into a \$10 million company," Ellison and Miner established a consulting business called Software Development Laboratories in a small office in Santa Clara.

It was while working on the CIA database that Ellison made a discovery that would change not only the company's direction, but the course of database design history. IBM had published a technical document describing a new method of "relational" (rather than hierarchical) data management and a programming language known as Structured Query Language (SQL), which was designed to tell a relational database what data to retrieve and how to display it. Applying his own experience to IBM's specifications, Ellison speedily implemented a relational database program, using SQL to enable users to extract corporate data in any form.

Like the Wizard of Oz, Ellison had (and still has) the uncanny ability to perceive what is already known in a different light, as well as the technological magic to bring that vision to reality. So it was that in 1979, the fledgling company released the world's first commercial SQL-based relational database management system (RDBMS)–two years ahead of IBM. That same year, the company name changed to Relational Software Incorporated. Ellison and Miner, who worked together to design and write the program, called their product "Oracle."

In retrospect, that name has proved prophetic for a company whose founders have demonstrated a 17-year oracular ability to predict the future–and with outstanding results. By April 1981, Oracle had gained 25 customers; by November 1981, that figure doubled to 50. A year later, Oracle had 100 customers. Today, nearly half of all installed relational database systems are Oracle.

By 1983, the program had become the premier information management software and the name "Oracle" had become synonymous with the company. Capitalizing on this identity, RSI changed its name to Oracle.

Another 1983 foresight–the need for open, distributed systems computing–led to Oracle's development of the first portable database. Since then, Oracle has continued to make its software portable and "hardware-agnostic" so that users can combine the power of an Oracle database with the flexibility to use whatever existing and changing hardware they desire. Today, Oracle software runs on over 70 platforms, including personal digital assistants (PDAs), PCs, minicomputers, mainframes, massively parallel processors (MPPs), and the television set-top boxes that will transform TVs into interactive devices on the information highway.

Growth and product expansion continued throughout the 1980s and into the 1990s. In 1984, the 100th employee was hired in the U.S., and Oracle introduced its first complete development "tool set," allowing anyone to develop applications accessing information stored in an Oracle database. In 1986, the company introduced the first client/server database. Meanwhile, Oracle's product line, platform base, customers, and revenues continued to climb. Sales and operating profits doubled every year. And of course, Oracle outgrew its facilities.

Co-founder Robert N. Miner shared in developing the Oracle system that gave the company its name

In 1978, the company moved from Santa Clara to Sand Hill Road in Menlo Park. Then, in 1990, Oracle relocated to its permanent site in Redwood City. The campus consists of five glistening cylindrical glass towers surrounding a man-made lake and lush green landscaping on what was once the site of the Marine World aquarium. Unlike the cookie-cutter, ground-hugging buildings typically favored by Silicon Valley companies, Oracle Headquarters rises majestically from the landscape and reflects all that surrounds it, symbolic of the visionary power of the company.

By the turn of the decade, Ellison again demonstrated the insight to realize that, with 50 products supported on 100 platforms, it was becoming difficult to guarantee 100% satisfaction with the company's technology once the customer got it home. He saw that the future hinged not only on high technology, but also on Oracle's ability to guide and support its customers in defining their computing environments. This created an additional focus in Oracle's operations on ensuring customers success in implementing Oracle's products. Today, nearly half of all Oracle employees hold customer-support positions in consulting and implementation services.

Still, Oracle remains a true technological visionary. What started back in 1977 with a vision of giving businesses better ways to manage and retrieve their information became a reality when Ellison and Miner delivered the world's first SQL-based relational database in 1979. Now a $3 billion powerhouse, Oracle is still worthy of its name, with new products and ingenious technology strategies to propel an eager world into the Information Age.

Ellison and his development team have already taken the lead by extending Oracle's core technology to store, manage, and distribute multimedia data-documents, video, audio, and images–in addition to traditional alphanumeric data. It is this Oracle technology that is powering the world's first real-life, working interactive television services, like video-on-demand, that will most likely become the everyday vehicles of the much-heralded information highway. And as the information highway begins to bring yet-to-be-imagined opportunities for electronic commerce, Oracle will once again help redefine the way companies do business.

Time and time again, Oracle has proven that behind the whiz-bang-whirl that emanates from its magical, mystical towers in Silicon Valley lives a team of technological wizards with the vision and chutzpah to lead the world through an exhilarating passage the Information Age–and beyond.

Hard-working Oracle employees play hard at their 1984 picnic

Apple Computer

Steve Wozniak and Steve Jobs show off the Apple I Board

When upstarts Steve Wozniak and Steve Jobs left Hewlett-Packard and Atari, respectively, in 1976, to form Apple Computer, they began a mission that has become a legacy: to change the way people use information to work, learn, and play. It began with a preassembled computer circuit board with no keyboard, case, sound, or graphics, and was initially sold to hobbyists. The Apple II and Apple III computer product families quickly followed. The introduction of the Macintosh computer in 1984 was a landmark in Apple's history–featuring point-and-click mouse control, menu-driven system navigation, and a small "footprint"–providing a personal computer that was as affordable as it was easy to use.

Apple's history is filled with industry-setting firsts. Apple innovated the mouse, icons, windows, menus, 3.5-inch floppy disks, and the phenomenon known as "desktop publishing." Most importantly, Apple was the first computer company to recognize the need for and the potential of personal computers–to market computers to the general public.

Their vision paid off. Apple quickly became a household name, went public in 1980 ($4.6 million in shares were gobbled up within minutes), became the first personal computer company to reach $1 billion in annual sales, had an installed base of over 650,000 units, and employed over 2,500 people worldwide. By then, the product line included low- and high-end versions of the Apple personal computer, several peripherals, and thousands of software programs.

The original Macintosh came with a built-in disk drive, 64K ROM, and a mouse. Price: $2,495

The mid-1980s was a turbulent but exciting era of growth, innovation, and change. Over 400,000 Macintosh computers were sold in the first year of production. That year, Apple also built the nation's most automated plant, featuring robotics, just-in-time delivery, and a linear assembly line.

Nineteen-eighty-five was the year Apple Computer grew up, with the pains and gains that come when a $2 billion multinational company undergoes a top-to-bottom reorganization. By year's end, founders Wozniak and Jobs had left the company. Though financially sound and dominant in education, government, and desktop publishing, Apple had still not achieved the penetration in the business sector it desired.

Then, Apple bettered its technical strengths (superior graphics and human interface), coupled them with a network solution as easy to learn and use as the Mac itself, and leveraged it as a turnkey solution for business. Apple quickly gained wide acceptance in technical and aerospace corporations, service companies, publishing, and large corporations.

Building on the company's fundamental principle that the individual, not the mainframe, belongs at the center of the computing universe, Apple continued to develop easy-to-use and affordable personal computing tools throughout the 1980s and into the 1990s. Apple introduced multitask, multimedia, and multiplatform capabilities. Then came portables and notebooks, new communications products, speech recognition, text-to-speech, video, and fax/modem capabilities.

In 1993, as Apple entered its 18th year, Michael Spindler replaced John Sculley as CEO of Apple Computer. In 1994, under Spindler's leadership, Apple introduced the Power Macintosh, the first Macintosh system based on the Power PC RISC microprocessor resulting from Apple's alliance with IBM and Motorola. The same year, Apple also announced an agreement with IBM and Motorola to develop a common hardware reference platform for RISC-based computers, in response to customers looking for solutions that are based on standards and that can be purchased from multiple vendors. In addition, Apple announced a strategy to broadly license the Macintosh operating system.

With its landmark approach to personal computing and its mission to change the way people use information to learn, work, and play, Apple Computer, Inc., has secured its rightful place in the history of Silicon Valley.

1987 Macintosh family portrait: The Mac Plus, Mac II and Mac SE

Quantum Corp.

"What really sets Quantum apart is our willingness to pursue the unconventional, to take a different path. We have a history of doing things differently — of looking for better ways."

— William J. (Bill) Miller
Former Chairman and CEO

Engineers including founders David Brown, seated, and Don Daniels, right, ponder problem in 1981

Founded in 1980, Quantum Corporation began operations in a rented corner of a helicopter plant in San Jose, California. In just one decade, the company grew to become one of the world's leading manufacturers of computer data storage devices.

Quantum shipped its first 3.5-inch hard disk drive in 1987. By 1993 Quantum was supplying original equipment manufacturers (OEMs) with more hard drives than any other company in the world. By the close of the company's fiscal year ended March 31, 1995, sales were $3.4 billion, and in August 1995, the company shipped its 50 millionth drive.

Quantum has set quality and technology standards as the mass storage industry advanced the art of packing larger and larger amounts of data into smaller and smaller devices. As competition in the mass storage industry increases and product cycles shrink, Quantum continues to provide major systems companies with leading-edge technology, the highest quality products, the right quantities at the right time, and a vision for the future that makes a difference to businesses and end-users alike.

To achieve these results and wide flexibility while responding to market changes, Quantum emphasizes automation and high yields. Matsushita Kotobuki Electronics (MKE, based in Japan, is a leader in robotics manufacturing) makes the bulk of Quantum's hard drives. A highly mechanized factory in Milpitas, California, produces Quantum's high-capacity products, with ranges beyond one gigabyte. Teaming up with MKE allows Quantum to focus on designing complex products and getting them to market quickly.

Strong OEM and distribution partnerships position Quantum for long-term growth in an often volatile marketplace. The company's largest OEM partners include Apple Computer, AST Research, Compaq, Dell Computer, Digital, Hewlett-Packard, and IBM.

In addition to its OEM base, Quantum markets its products through a domestic and international network of commercial and industrial distributors that includes more than 25 countries in North America, Western and Eastern Europe, Japan, the Asia-Pacific region, and Latin America. The company maintains a consistent corporate focus on the unique needs of partners and the distribution channel by offering programs that lead to strong, lasting business relationships.

As a result of the October 1994 acquisition of Digital Equipment Corporation's storage division, Quantum's products have evolved from a successful line of high-performance, high-quality 5.25-inch, 3.5-inch, and 2.5-inch hard disk drives to include solid state disks, mid-range tapes (DLT™), and thin film heads. This significant acquisition positioned Quantum even more solidly as the world's mass storage leader by broadening the company's technology portfolio, increasing development resources, and providing direct access to magnetoresistive technology.

In September 1995, Michael A. Brown, 37, moved up to the post of Quantum chief executive officer.

Based in Milpitas, with over 10,000 employees worldwide, Quantum Corporation designs and manufactures storage products for today's digitized world. The company is well-positioned to take advantage of exciting future opportunities based on its broad product line, deep technology portfolio, and strength of customer relationships.

In 1995, Quantum shipped its 50 millionth disk drive

1981
Egyptian president Anwar Sadat is assassinated.

1982
Israeli forces invade southern Lebanon; massacre of Palestinians in Beirut refugee camp.

War between Argentina and Britain (Falklands War).

1983
Conflict in Sudan; so far more than 1.5 million people have died

Sally Ride blasts off on six-day Challenger flight.

U.S.S.R. shoots down Korean Air Lines passenger plane.

Sun Microsystems founders

Chapter 13: Microcomputers Fuel Expansion

In 1981, International Business Machines Corp. entered the personal computer market, and was welcomed as a competitor, rather slyly, by Apple. IBM's PC boasted a disk operating system that became an industry standard. Hewlett-Packard had launched its first PC in 1980. The early '80s were to be dominated by microcomputer expansions — and by a torrid pace of start-ups.

Steadily improving microprocessors triggered a related explosion of other peripherals: printers, modems, disk drives, interlinked networks, equipment for building chips, video games, computer-assisted design. The games business reached its zenith in 1981 and by 1983 was plummeting.

The race to gain share in the expanding PC market created a profusion of new models, some of them tardy though much ballyhooed — a phenomenon scornfully called "vaporware." In 1983, IBM introduced its PC-XT, the first personal computer with a built-in (10-megabit) hard drive. Meanwhile, Compaq marketed a "clone" of an IBM PC, starting production of a flood of IBM compatibles by rivals trying to improve on and/or undersell the industry standard-bearer.

Apple offered an expensive model called the Lisa in 1983, and it flopped. Recovering in 1984, Apple introduced the Macintosh to instant popularity. The Mac made affordable innovations that had been part of the Lisa, such as pull-down menus and the mouse as an alternative to moving the cursor with keystrokes. The Mac's special graphics capabilities endeared it to illustrators and designers.

Computer-assisted design (CAD) took off after invention of the silicon compiler in 1979. Former Stanford professor James H. Clark founded Silicon Graphics in 1982 to develop three-dimensional computer graphics and marketed the first 3-D workstation in 1984. Edward McCracken later replaced Clark as Silicon Graphics CEO.

Another 1982 start-up was Sun Microsystems, also born in a Stanford laboratory. Sun founders Andreas Bechtolsheim, Scott McNealy, and Vinod Khosla, abetted by Stanford professor Forest Baskett, saw potential for workstations able to share data using the UNIX operating system favored by scientists and engineers. McNealy became the CEO.

Daisywheel and dot-matrix printers, the early choices, began to give way in 1984 when Hewlett-Packard pioneered inkjet technology.

John Warnock and Charles Geschke led a group of former Xerox PARC scientists in founding Adobe Systems in 1982. They aimed to develop a standard computer language that would consistently transmit even the most complex pages

3-D rendering

Adobe Systems meeting

to a printer. Their scalable-font software product, PostScript, eventually became the industry standard.

Another 1982 start-up, Cypress Semiconductors, began when a group of CMOS (complementary metal oxide semiconductor) engineers led by TJ Rodgers deemed Advanced Micro Devices too slow to adopt that technology and programmable gate arrays. CMOS, as the Japanese had learned, proved to be a "slow and low" (low-powered) answer for small battery-driven electronic devices such as notebook computers, and Cypress found a niche at the high end of the customized chip market.

Xilinx entered the customizing arena in 1984 to create field-programmable gate arrays, enabling buyers to customize computer instructions to fit their own needs. Bernie Vonderschmitt, Ross Freeman, and Jim Barnett, former Zilog employees, were its founders.

Another 1984 start-up is Cisco Systems, founded by a husband-and-wife team, Leonard Bosack and Sandra Lerner. Cisco used technology Bosack had developed to link Stanford computers so he and his bride-to-be could communicate, though in separate departments. Later in the '80s, when the market for network routers opened up, Cisco was ready.

Cirrus Logic also made its debut in 1984, adapting an efficient chip developed by Suhas Patil to the first controllers built directly on a disk drive. This led to the PC industry's shift to smaller disk drives. Sybase, Inc., entered the high-performance relational database management field in 1984 in competition with Oracle Systems and became a significant player in the 1990s.

Although U.S. firms had controlled the semiconductor memory market throughout the 1970s, 1984 brought a startling reversal as Japanese producers moved into an early lead and went on to capture all of the 256K DRAM market, thus dominating the latest development. Wails that Silicon Valley had lost its edge began to make headlines.

Stanford professor Henry Taube won the 1983 Nobel Prize for chemistry for new discoveries in the basic mechanism of chemical reactions. One application of his findings has been in selecting metallic compounds for use as superconductors.

The U.S. space shuttle grabbed the manned-flight spotlight, with Columbia beginning operational missions late in 1982. Challenger first flew in 1983, Discovery in 1984.

Space shuttle Columbia

1984

Sikhs assassinate Indira Gandhi, Indian prime minister.

New Zealand declared a nuclear-free zone.

Failure of rain dependent crops after extensive drought causing famine in Africa. First acknowledgment of famine in Ethiopia, Sudan, and Chad by the west.

Attempt by the IRA to assassinate British cabinet.

Charles Geschke is co-founder and president of Adobe Systems

Who started desktop publishing? Whatever part anyone else played, the essential key to this revolutionary innovation was development of a standard computer language and scalable-font software by John Warnock and Charles Geschke at Adobe Systems in the early 1980s.

The two men teamed up in 1978 at the Xerox Palo Alto Research Center when Geschke, a veteran researcher in programming languages, set up a new Imaging Sciences Laboratory and hired Warnock, a longtime computer graphics innovator, as chief scientist. Developing research with broad applicability in electronic printing, they spent two years "selling" a standard within Xerox, only to have it put under wraps. Frustrated, they decided to go into business on their own and founded Adobe Systems in Mountain View in 1982. The name came from the creek that runs near their Los Altos area homes.

Although never formal partners, Warnock and Geschke—both personable, bearded scientists with doctorates and outlooks so alike that they never argue—have etched a place among such famed electronics duos as Boole and Babbage, Hewlett and Packard, Jobs and Wozniak.

Their business plan did not call for reinventing the electronic printing standard; instead, it envisioned producing a turnkey collection of hardware and software to sell to corporate publishers. Six other companies—all vanished now—had similar ideas. When Warnock and Geschke found that the printing technology they had devised was in high demand, they gave up the turnkey systems notion and did reinvent the standard. Their page-description language, PostScript™, communicates precise descriptions of computer-generated graphics, photos, and text to any output device with an Adobe PostScript interpreter.

Warnock, Geschke, and Xerox PARC colleagues who joined them in founding Adobe adopted atypical policies for the start-up. They gave liberal stock options to everyone joining the company. They sought to work smart and leverage their resources while resisting the 80-hour, 7-day workweeks, and other intense pressures that burn out engineers at many start-ups. "We tried to even out our development and set reasonable targets and objectives, so people did not have to destroy their personal lives in order to make the company a success," Geschke said.

PostScript was first marketed in 1985. Before that, however, Adobe got a big break. Steve Jobs of Apple Computer visited Adobe and, as Warnock tells it, "we showed him what we were doing and he said, 'This is exactly what we need for the Macintosh,' and that's the way the Laserwriter was born. ... In retrospect, Apple's dominance of the desktop publishing arena is due primarily to that Laserwriter and those early discussions."

Adobe Illustrator made its debut in 1987, simplifying creation, manipulation, and refinement of artwork, with advanced features for editing, text handling, and color support. This product was followed in 1989 by Photoshop, an "electronic darkroom."

In September 1989, two dominant companies in the personal computer industry posed a threat to Adobe's very future. At a Seybold conference on the publishing arts, Apple Computer and Microsoft said in effect that they were out to bury Adobe. Apple said it would license True Type fonts to Microsoft; Microsoft said it would license a PostScript Interpreter it had to Apple.

Adobe, although shaken, rose to the challenge. The company already had an open standard for Type 1 fonts and its Adobe PostScript Interpreter. The open standard was extended to cover its font format, so other software and hardware companies could access and use the hitherto closely guarded technology for controlling how typefaces and other images are created on printers and computer screens. Shortly afterward, the company announced its Adobe Type Manager, a software utility that eliminates jagged type on the computer screen and printed page, enabling Macintosh and Windows users to scale Type 1 fonts to any size and print them at the highest possible resolution.

In the struggle for control of desktop publishing software technology, IBM decided not to take sides. Then Apple junked its licensing agreement with Microsoft and signed up to use Adobe's interpreter in Macintosh upgrades. Finally , in June 1991, Microsoft said uncle and disbanded its printer business unit, although it continues to use True Type fonts licensed

Adobe's PostScript language and font family line up for review

Adobe Photoshop, introduced in 1989, enables graphic artists to do "electronic darkroom" work on images

from Apple in its Windows operating systems. Adobe had fought off the attacks on its niche.

That niche, by the way, is no small one. "People don't realize it," Warnock explained, "but the technology that we developed in the early '80s and the desktop publishing revolution have really taken over all of printing and publishing. So every newspaper today, every magazine, every product brochure, every advertisement you see in every magazine uses a piece of our technology, and uses our type library, and uses the graphic arts interface. Every cereal box on the shelf, the titling on a lot of television channels—they all use it."

Adobe has poured out a steady stream of new and upgraded products. In August 1994, Aldus Corporation of Seattle, Washington, and Adobe merged under the Adobe name. Aldus— started in 1984 by newspaper executive Paul Brainerd and named for Renaissance publisher Aldus Manutius—also had helped to launch desktop publishing. In 1985, Aldus brought out PageMaker, an international leader in offering tools for persons in the publishing cycle who produce professional-quality materials: graphic artists and designers, writers, editors, and typesetters, production artists, and prepress professionals. Users can integrate text and graphics from many sources into virtually any kind of printed document. Ex-Aldus operations continue in Seattle.

In 1993, the company introduced a major innovation: Adobe Acrobat, a family of software products that allow fully formatted, electronic documents—containing distinctive typefaces, color, graphics, and photographs—to be easily distributed, accessed, and reused, regardless of the hardware platform, operating system, or application used to create the original.

Another acquisition announced in mid-1995 promises to bring Frame Technology's document management skills, particularly for UNIX platforms, under Adobe's tent. Indeed, Frame's San Jose base is just across the street from a high-rise building where Adobe plans to consolidate its headquarters. Like Adobe, Frame has worked to make document transfer across platforms of all sorts seamless, and the two companies had collaborated on several projects before their merger was negotiated.

Today, Adobe is the premier supplier of information authoring and management tools that enable people to make, send, find, view, and print visually rich content.

Adobe has manufacturing facilities located in California. Manufacturing operations involve the duplication of disks, assembly of purchased parts, and final packaging for application and type products. Some manufacturing activities are contracted to third parties, primarily in Europe. The company went public in 1986 (NASDAQ:ADBE.) Worldwide, it had 1,584 employees as of late November 1994. Adobe's 1994 revenues totaled $597.7 million.

John Warnock is co-founder, chairman and CEO of Adobe Systems

Company founders joined in hand assembly of early Sun-1 workstation, c.1983

*S*un Microsystems, Inc. has proven that if you build it—and it shines—they will come. When the company was launched in 1982 by four 27-year-old men on a mission to provide "open" desktop computers at one-tenth the cost of existing systems, no one realized it was the beginning of a revolution. Not only did their product strategy defy conventional thinking, so did their management "style." Sun wanted to have fun—while producing low-cost, high-performance computer systems using off-the-shelf parts. This seemingly incongruent vision led competitors, primarily conservative East Coast companies, to respond to Sun's burst onto the market with a dismissing pass of the hand and the comment, "Everything loose rolls to the West Coast."

It didn't take long before these detractors found themselves in Sun's shadow. By its second birthday, Sun had grown to more than 400 employees and annual sales of $39 million. At the tender age of 5, revenues had soared to $500 million. On its 10th birthday in 1992, Sun stood at more than 12,500 employees and more than $3.5 billion in sales.

Sun's brilliance can be traced to its enlightened beginning. The year was 1981. Stanford graduate student Andreas (Andy) Bechtolsheim, frustrated at having to go to the campus computer center whenever he needed a powerful system, designed a workstation for himself using standard parts. He soon began licensing his new computer, called the Sun (Stanford University Network), for $10,000 a pop.

Sun ATM adapter board made its debut in 1995

Bechtolsheim had a dream. Inspired by his prior experience with Xerox's fabled Palo Alto Research Center (PARC), where the concept of easy-to-use, networked desktop computers was born, he envisioned an "open" system that would run on UNIX®. He used $25,000 of his own money to build prototypes. Demand for the system was strong, attracting the attention of Stanford MBA graduate Vinod Khosla, a native of India with a burning desire to retire a millionaire by the age of 30.

Khosla had just left Daisy, a CAE pioneer he helped found in 1980, because he felt the industry needed a general purpose workstation. Khosla believed Bechtolsheim's machine held that promise, but he wanted more than the "golden egg"—he wanted the goose that laid it. He convinced Bechtolsheim to join him in building a "big company."

Next, over a hamburger at a Palo Alto McDonald's, Khosla recruited Scott McNealy, a fellow Stanford MBA with an economics degree from Harvard, to head up Sun's manufacturing. The son of an American Motors executive, McNealy immediately saw the promise in Sun—and the opportunity to change the fundamentals of the computer industry the same way Henry Ford changed those of the automobile industry.

Then, they reeled in the only clear choice to head the company's software efforts. Bill Joy was already widely known as the leading light in the UNIX world (he was principal architect and designer for UC Berkeley's version of UNIX). He became the final cornerstone of Sun's founding team.

This foursome started the company on a mission that remains today: to continually build better, faster, and cheaper products; to succeed in the tumultuous computer world through creativity; to maintain nonconventional ways of thinking ... and to have fun in the process. They have succeeded on all counts.

Just three months after Sun was founded, manufacturing commenced and the first products were shipped. The cofounders and a handful of employees assembled the first few hundred units mostly by hand. Soon, however, Sun settled into a product philosophy it follows to this day: off-the-shelf components and streamlined designs, resulting in quick time-to-market and low prices. Within six months, the company became profitable.

The Sun-1™ and subsequent Sun-2™ workstations were instant successes, with 80% of the first year's $8 million in sales coming

Scott McNealy, age 30, beams Sun's success in 1985 soon after becoming president

from the university markets. Just 17 months after incorporation, Sun began to aggressively pursue new markets. One of their first targets was ComputerVision, a major CAD supplier. Although CV initially chose Apollo, the Sun team made an eleventh-hour offer CV couldn't refuse, putting Sun on the map in the mainstream technical market.

By then Sun had outgrown its original facilities in Santa Clara and had moved to a larger building in Mountain View. As the company grew, it expanded into adjacent buildings. Sun continued to foster a high-energy yet playful corporate culture that offered professional challenge but also fun. Friday beer busts and Wednesday donut days became fixtures.

Another tradition established early was an annual April Fool's prank, with such stunts as placing Joy's Ferrari on a platform in the middle of a pond within Sun's "campus" one year, and disassembling and reassembling an entire Volkswagen Beetle inside an executive's office the next.

Worker tests columns of material for workstations at Sun plant in 1987

This seemingly casual environment, however, belied the fact that Sun was rapidly becoming a major player. The first European office opened in January 1984, and later that year, Sun launched a subsidiary, Sun Federal, to serve the government market. New products were introduced every few months. And Sun continued to champion (almost singularly) open systems, designing and licensing NFS file sharing software that soon became the industry standard. That same year, McNealy became president.

By the mid-'80s, the market had begun to embrace the open systems concept. While competitors hedged and hawed, Sun continued to make rapid gains in important technical market segments. In 1986, the company went public. In 1987, Sun streaked past Apollo in sales, with a 146% increase in revenues from the previous year. A year later, Sun hit $1 billion in annual sales.

In 1987, Sun introduced a new computer based on RISC technology, the SPARC™ system. This small, inexpensive, desktop moved Sun beyond the technical stronghold into the enormous commercial markets. No longer could even the giants of the computer industry dismiss Sun as a harmless little West Coast company with "loose" strategies. Not only was Sun a contender, it was a leader.

Displays on graphics and imaging board show what a SPARC system can do

As the open systems revolt picked up further steam in the '90s, virtually every company began to rewrite its product strategies. Sun simply refined theirs. In 1990, with 39% of the worldwide workstation and server shipments, Sun overtook the "big boys" to claim the number one position.

By 1991, Sun had long since become the "big company" the founders had envisioned. In order to remain quick and nimble, Sun Microsystems reorganized into smaller subsidiaries, with each unit focusing on a core business and operating as a separate profit and loss center. Yet, the essence of the company hasn't changed. The facilities and people are basically the same. The quest to introduce low-cost, innovative products remains, as evidenced by the release of SVR4 (Solaris®), developed in partnership with AT&T and considered the premier UNIX operating system today. Sun continues to be fueled by creativity and financial acumen. And they're still having fun, even as they reach for the Sun to become a $10 billion industry leader.

"Fabless" in reaching its $1 billion revenue run rate, Cirrus Logic now produces wafers together with IBM

When Mike Hackworth got together with Suhas Patil in 1984, he thought he might be able to use the software Patil had invented: a Storage/Logic Array program for very large scale integration (VLSI) design. Hackworth, then a senior vice president at Signetics (now Philips Semiconductor), was frustrated by the many months and great effort it was taking to bring out the new VLSI chips. Patil, a former MIT professor, had a new technique that got around the many problems encountered with gate arrays or standard cells, but he needed a partner to help move his start-up to the next stage.

The two men hit it off, and Hackworth agreed to become a mentor to Patil Systems. Then came a revelation. "When I fully understood the power of Suhas' software, it hit me like a ton of bricks that his design approach could be the basis for a new kind of chip company," Hackworth said. "I could see the opportunity to get complex chips out in just six months using system designers who didn't require a knowledge of silicon. I got excited about hiring system engineers accustomed to designing at the board or box level, and having them use Patil's software to innovate system-level chips."

The possibilities persuaded Hackworth to leave his top-echelon post at Signetics and join Patil. Since January 1985, he has been president and chief executive officer of Cirrus Logic. Patil is chairman of the board and executive vice president for products and technology. On a day-to-day basis, the two men work as partners running a rapidly growing business.

Hackworth led in shaping the strategy that has rocketed Cirrus Logic to a billion-dollar-a-year run rate faster than any other Silicon Valley semiconductor firm ever made that climb—and without a fab of its own. The company ranks as a leading manufacturer of advanced integrated circuits and related software for multimedia, communications, system logic and mass storage in personal computers. It doesn't make CPUs or memories, but its chips fill the most demanding peripheral needs on a PC motherboard. Cirrus Logic sometimes calls them "all the other computers inside."

Hackworth's daughter Lauren suggested the company's name. Cirrus, the highest clouds in the sky, she thought, might symbolize the high-level designs the company would create.

Since its founding, Cirrus Logic's strategy has been to anticipate transitions in large existing and emerging growth markets, and create system-level solutions ahead of those transitions to capture market leadership. This strategy is supported by an expanding base of key technologies and above-average R&D investments (historically more than 18% of sales). A series of acquisitions has also served to expand the company's portfolio of products and technologies.

Although often seen as a provider of mass storage chips that jumped nimbly into other markets later, Cirrus Logic's original business plan called for developing chips for PC graphics and communications as well as mass storage. Interestingly, the company's very first product—code-named "starfish"—was a cable TV converter chip. This early "set-top" converter chip became the company's first product to reach the million-unit shipping milestone.

Shortly after Hackworth joined forces with Patil, the newly organized management team spotted an approaching market transition in mass storage. Until 1987, controller cards were separate from the hard disks they ruled, but Cirrus Logic observed that their functions could be embedded within the hard disk drive itself. The company pioneered Integrated Drive Electronics (IDE), and ever since has been a leading supplier of hard-disk controller chips.

Next came graphics. Cirrus Logic engineers were designing a display graphics controller in 1987 when IBM announced its new Video Graphics Array (VGA) technology standard. They quickly showed samples of a VGA controller at a trade show a few months later. Again Cirrus Logic took an early lead and held it. More than half the desktop PCs shipped today contain its

Cirrus Logic pioneers gather in 1985 to formulate strategic growth plans

graphics controllers and accelerators.

Anticipating the evolution of the PC from a word processing and spreadsheet focus to a multimedia and communications platform, Cirrus Logic led the industry in the integration of both graphics and video functions on the same chip. Moreover, it introduced a controller chip that connected CD-ROM drives directly to PCs without needing costly adapter circuitry.

Cirrus Logic added a VGA controller for flat panel liquid crystal displays (LCDs), giving the emerging notebook PC market a strong boost back in 1989. The company later offered "power on demand" system logic to prolong notebook battery life and deal with heat generated by advanced microprocessors. In addressing the growing mobile computing market, Cirrus Logic helped define the PC Card (formerly PCMCIA) standard for connecting optional credit card-size devices to portables; about half the portables sold use its host adapters.

Communications took the longest to unfold. Cirrus Logic ranks as one of the top three suppliers of fax/data modem chip sets, and now is integrating voice as well. The company has also made significant strides in the wireless communications market.

Eight acquisitions since 1990 have amplified and complemented Cirrus Logic's core skills. A good example is PCSI of San Diego, which functions as an independent subsidiary. An emerging leader in the digital wireless market, PCSI makes chips and systems that enable Cellular Digital Packet Data (CDPD) communications. CDPD transforms the idle time on analog cellular voice systems into wireless channels that carry digital data. PCSI also markets digital cordless telephone chip sets.

Crystal Semiconductor of Austin, Texas also functions as an independent subsidiary, producing analog and mixed-signal products for multimedia audio and data acquisition. Crystal has emerged the undisputed market leader in bringing CD quality audio to PCs with its family of codecs. Other acquisitions, notably Pixel Semiconductor (video processors) and PicoPower Technology (system logic), have been merged into Cirrus Logic's headquarter operations in Fremont, California.

Throughout its swift ascent, Cirrus Logic has operated as a fabless company, utilizing production capacity of other companies and focusing its investments in new product R&D rather than in building costly fabrication clean rooms. At the company's present size and scale of operations, however, that is beginning to change. Cirrus Logic and IBM Corporation now share ownership of a company named MiCRUS with a fab in East Fishkill, N.Y. Production of Cirrus Logic wafers began there during the first quarter of 1995—essentially after a fabless Cirrus Logic reached its billion-dollar run rate.

A rarity in Silicon Valley, Hackworth is a local boy. While attending Serra High School in San Mateo and Santa Clara University, he worked for Ultronix, a passive components start-up. Before his 14-year stint at Signetics, he filled marketing and sales management posts at Fairchild Semiconductor and Motorola. His life experiences have inspired him to make Cirrus Logic an exemplary corporate citizen within Silicon Valley. The company is an ardent supporter and sponsor of numerous community programs, including Junior Achievement, the Tech Museum of Innovation, Boston's Computer Museum, the Children's Shelter, the San Jose Symphony, the San Jose Cleveland Ballet, the Silicon Valley Charity Ball and the Second Harvest Food Bank, among others.

Hackworth often speaks of building "the Next Great American Semiconductor Company." Cirrus Logic's impressive track record in capturing leading market positions clearly imparts that potential. In its tested style, the company anticipates that the increasing convergence of computing, communications, and consumer electronics will create myriad opportunities for its expanding portfolio of technologies and products.

Mike Hackworth (left) and Suhas Patil, partners in leading Cirrus Logic

Xilinx, Inc.

Bernie Vonderschmitt, Xilinx co-founder and chief executive

Xilinx, Inc., the company that pioneered field programmable gate arrays (FPGAs), has in the past decade firmly established itself as the world's leading supplier of programmable logic. Programmable logic products are semiconductors manufactured as commodity (standard) devices which can be personalized (customized) by Electronic Design Automation software.

The company was founded in 1984, one of a cluster of semiconductor businesses formed by brilliant engineers frustrated because their managements refused or were slow to exploit promising technologies they had conceptualized. It is a Silicon Valley conundrum whether this sort of entrepreneurial thrust is unstoppable, or whether top company executives and financiers can ever learn the lesson that spin-off-starters have taught repeatedly through fabulous successes.

Xilinx sprang from the urges of three engineers who were employed by Zilog, a chip maker. One of them, Ross Freeman, was convinced that an off-the-shelf logic product, if it does many things for many people, is better than a customized device. Freeman believed a product could be developed that would allow buyers to do their own adapting of integrated circuits for their own particular requirements.

Freeman had designed one hit product for Zilog and helped design another, and he'd been promoted to director of IC engineering. Managing 200 people had left him too busy to indulge his own drive to design.

Two other engineers, Bernie Vonderschmitt and Jim Barnett, joined with Freeman in founding Xilinx in 1984. Late in his long career, Vonderschmitt, then 60, had developed an impatience akin to Freeman's. After spending 25 years working with RCA on the East Coast in solid-state electronics, Vonderschmitt decided RCA had lost its interest in cutting-edge technology, adding: "I left after they bought a consumer finance company." He returned to college full-time to take an MBA degree, then moved to California and was hired by Zilog to run the microprocessor operation in Campbell. Zilog was a tiny subsidiary of the giant Exxon Corp., and Vonderschmitt and the others got nowhere when they asked the corporation to put up some funds to develop Freeman's idea. "They weren't interested," Vonderschmitt says.

So the three engineers formed Xilinx, and Freeman succeeded in developing and patenting a logic cell array, also called a programmable gate array.

Inventive new architecture marked Xilinx's first product, the XC2064 family—at 10 times today's FPGA cost

They already had gone after venture capital, scoring with several of the biggest names in start-up finance. Hambrecht & Quist, J.H. Whitney, and Kleiner Perkins Caufield and Byers put up $4.25 million to start Xilinx. Vonderschmitt headed the firm.

By 1985, the company marketed the first field programmable gate array. Now the customer, rather than the chip factory, could program the thousands of openable gates so as to define a custom integrated circuit. It was a CMOS device, but Freeman liked to point out that Xilinx was a programmable gate array company, not a CMOS gate array company. He anticipated other technologies that would later become available.

The difficult years of the 1980s made it hard for Xilinx to gain momentum, but it gradually did, enough to survive Freeman's untimely death in 1989. In 1990, the company went public (NASDAQ:XLNX); Barnett departed in the same year, but Vonderschmitt continued to run the company with gusto as a senior statesman of the semiconductor world.

Part of the Xilinx strategy has been to operate as a fabless manufacturer, farming out production to fabrication plants in Japan. Not needing to invest in a costly fab of its own, the company spent heavily on research and development, increasing the outlay every year, to a level of $45 million in FY 1995. Gross profit is high in this chipmaking arena: over 60% of revenues for Xilinx.

Successor products to the first FPGAs, the XC2000 family introduced in 1985, had increased gateway densities: more than 5,000 usable logic gates in the XC3000 (1987) and up to 20,000 in the XC4000 (1990). From 1987 to 1992, Xilinx regularly cut prices by about 30% each year. Vonderschmitt has steadily pursued a strategy of narrowing the cost differential between programmable and mask-programmed chips. Manufacturers had a habit of using Xilinx chips to launch a product and then, if it succeeded, switching to custom-designed chips that were much

Ross Freeman, co-founder of Xilinx and inventor of the programmable gate array

cheaper at high volume. To allay such defections, Xilinx now offers its own HardWire™ LCA™ products, which enable the same transition with many fewer steps.

After acquisition in 1993 of Plus Logic, another Silicon Valley programmable logic company, Xilinx brought out a new kind of programmable logic chip based on EPROM (electrically programmable read only memory) cells. Still another technology, called anti-fuse, has been developed by Xilinx. Because of patents, related to FPGAs, held by Xilinx and Actel, another FPGA manufacturer, the two companies concluded a cross-licensing agreement several years ago. This agreement minimizes any future litigation between the two companies.

The March 1995 merger with NeoCAD, a Boulder, Colorado-based developer of high performance design software for FPGAs, has enabled Xilinx to introduce a new wave of products in FY 1996. These provide increased performance, density, and software that enables extracting the optimum in price, performance, and density. Although software is a relatively small segment of the company's business, Xilinx deems it important to cost reduction and a key to improving performance for customers.

The company's products serve a base of more than 5,000 customers worldwide. Approximately 60% of the North American sales come from data processing, datacom, telecom, and networking applications; the remainder is split among industrial and instrumentation products, military uses, and other assorted applications.

As an established supplier to all segments of the emerging global communications network, Xilinx sees the digital highway as heading in its direction.

In 1994, Curt Wozniak, who had spent more than 10 years in senior management positions with Sun Microsystems, joined Xilinx at corporate headquarters in San Jose as president and chief operating officer. Vonderschmitt, now in his early 70s and still obviously relishing his role in building a fast-growing company, continues as chief executive officer.

During the fiscal year that ended March 31, 1995, Xilinx rolled up sales of $355.1 million, virtually double the company's revenues two years earlier. At the year-end, Xilinx had 868 employees.

During calendar 1994, Xilinx became the world's largest supplier of programmable logic products, surpassing Advanced Micro Devices. Vonderschmitt and Wozniak have announced their intention to double Xilinx' number of product architectures in FY 1996. The company is also moving many of its existing product families to more advanced process technologies in order to reduce costs and improve performance. Xilinx is well-positioned for continued success as this vigorous and innovative company approaches the millennium.

Today Xilinx offers over 750 product variations with densities well beyond 25,000 gates

Silicon Graphics, Inc.

Silicon Graphics product array features set of high-performance visual computing systems

Imagine Silicon Valley during its agricultural heyday. Travel back to the time of the Spanish explorers, of the Ohlones, then far back to the Jurassic age. Now, fast forward to the future, to the 21st century. Today, with the visual computing products provided by Silicon Graphics, Inc., you can actually see inconceivable ideas—from dinosaurs to DNA —as 3-D color images, and interact with them in real time.

Silicon Graphics pioneered three-dimensional computing and has become the leading supplier of high-performance visual computing systems for technical, scientific, and creative professionals. The company was founded in 1982 by James H. Clark, a former Stanford University professor who with a graduate student, Marc Hannah, developed a custom chip called the Geometry Engine to handle complex 3-D graphics.

At the time, visual computing was largely viewed as a specialty niche for advanced technical and scientific uses. But Silicon Graphics' founders foresaw that visual computing could enhance productivity in a wide range of applications. Today, the technology that Silicon Graphics spearheaded is an acknowledged user productivity tool in scientific, technical, business, and creative computing environments.

The company's strengths include high-performance graphics, multiprocessing, digital media (sound and video), and RISC CPU technologies. Silicon Graphics customers span a wide variety of applications and industries—including scientific visualization, manufacturing, CAD/CAM, chemistry, molecular modeling, visual simulation, architectural design, virtual reality, animation, rendering, game development, and special effects. The company has also expanded into database, data mining, publishing, and interactive television markets, and authoring and serving solutions for the Internet's World Wide Web.

The company's IRIS 1000 Graphics Terminal was released in 1983. In 1988, the IRIS POWER Series, the first symmetric multiprocessing computer, was introduced. Silicon Graphics has unveiled many technology breakthroughs over the years, including the world's fastest interactive high-end graphics (RealityEngine), the first interactive digital cable TV system (in conjunction with Time Warner Cable), and the first desktop system with a digital color video camera (Indy).

Edward R. McCracken, a former Hewlett-Packard executive, joined Silicon Graphics in 1984 as president and chief executive officer. Ten years later, McCracken succeeded Clark as chairman; he continues as chairman and CEO.

In February 1993, President Bill Clinton and Vice President Al Gore visited the company's headquarters in Mountain View, and used the site to announce the administration's technology policy—an event providing global recognition of Silicon Valley as high technology's heartland.

The landscape of technology continues to change. In 1992, Silicon Graphics merged with MIPS Computer Systems, thus securing the future of the microprocessor technology used in its computers. Independent subsidiary Silicon Studio was established in 1994 to better serve the entertainment community. Interactive Digital Solutions, a joint venture with AT&T Network and Time Warner Cable, was formed that year to deliver the promise of interactive digital television. And in 1995, Silicon Graphics merged with Alias Research and Wave Technologies to form a wholly owned independent software subsidiary to develop the world's most advanced tools for creating digital content.

Silicon Graphics employs more than 5,900 people worldwide. In 1994, the company soared past the $1 billion revenue milestone, and its rapid growth continues.

What digital technology can accomplish has increased tenfold in just three years, McCracken has said, adding: "We are the center of the world in our ability to do this.This market won't mature until well into the 21st century."

Thus Silicon Graphics is poised, as the master of innovation at the crossroads of converging technologies, to define the computing landscape of the new millennium.

Image of space flight was created on Silicon Graphics 3-D computer using Alias Power Animator

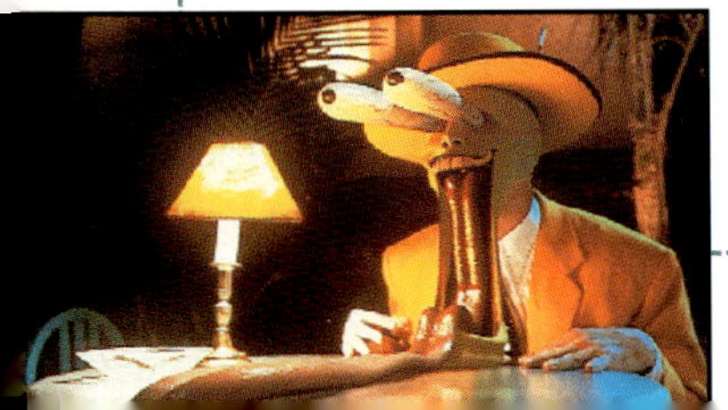

Scene from The Mask, a 1994 movie, shows creative wizardry of several Bay Area companies

Gordon E. Eubanks Jr. has served as Symantec's president and chief executive since 1984

Symantec is a global computer software company with an ever-expanding product line. Best known as the industry leader in desktop utility software for PC and Macintosh platforms, the company has recently broadened its offerings to include products for local-area and wide-area computer networks. Today, Symantec offers network and desktop products in three categories: development tools, utilities, and productivity applications.

Dr. Gary Hendrix, one of America's leading experts in artificial intelligence and natural language processing, founded Symantec in 1982. Gordon E. Eubanks Jr., founder of C&E Software, acquired Symantec in 1984, and continues as president and CEO.

The company has grown rapidly through the success of its products and a series of 17 acquisitions resulting in a broad line of business and productivity solutions. The acquisitions have strongly influenced the company's innovative organization. With corporate headquarters in Cupertino, California, where finance, sales, and marketing are centralized, Symantec has major software development sites at Beaverton, Oregon; Santa Monica and Novato, California; Huntington, New York; and Bedford, Massachusetts. International operations are located in Australia, New Zealand, Canada, France, Germany, Holland, Ireland, Italy, Japan, Taiwan, Russia, and the United Kingdom.

In 1985, Symantec released Q&A®, an award-winning flat-file database and word processing software for the IBM PC. Recognizing that software was also being created by small entrepreneurial developers, Symantec formed Turner Hall Publishing, a division devoted to publishing third-party software. In October 1985, Turner Hall introduced Note-It®, a notation utility for Lotus 1-2-3.

Acquisitions in 1987 were Breakthrough Software, developer of Time Line®, a leading project management program (IBM); Living Videotext, developer of ThinkTank, the predecessor to MORE, a presentation graphics software program (Macintosh); and THINK Technologies, which had developed THINK C and THINK Pascal programming languages (Macintosh).

Symantec went public in 1989 (NASDAQ:SYMC).

In 1990, Symantec acquired Peter Norton Computing, Inc. Peter Norton founded his company in 1982 and introduced Norton Utilities® software, the PC utilities market leader.

Three more acquisitions followed in 1991: Leonard Development Group, developer of Great Works, an integrated Macintosh program; Zortech, Inc., developer of cross-platform C++ compilers; and Dynamic Microprocessor Associates, Inc., developer of pcANYWHERE® software, the leading remote control communications software product.

Acquisitions continued in 1992 with Symantec U.K., a distributor; The Whitewater Group, developer of object-oriented programming tools and class libraries; MultiScope, Inc., which developed debuggers for Windows, DOS, and OS/2; and Certus, which created security and antivirus software for the PC.

In 1993, Symantec acquired Contact Software International, Inc., the developer of ACT!® software, the leading contact management package; and Fifth Generation Systems, Inc., developer of Fast Back®, DiskLock®, and other utility products. The company also bought technology from two companies to complement its expanding focus on client/server applications.

In 1994, Symantec bought a major competitor, Central Point Software, Inc., a developer of desktop utility and network management software, along with SLR Systems, Inc., a developer of third-party development products, and Intec Systems Inc., a developer of enterprise-wide mobile computing platforms.

For FY 1995, Symantec posted total revenues of $334.9 million. The company is committed to maintaining a high level of investment in product research and development.

With its unique position as the leader in desktop and enterprise utilities, and its strength in application development and productivity products, Symantec is well poised for the future.

Peter Norton's popular Norton Utilities is one of Symantec's software sets

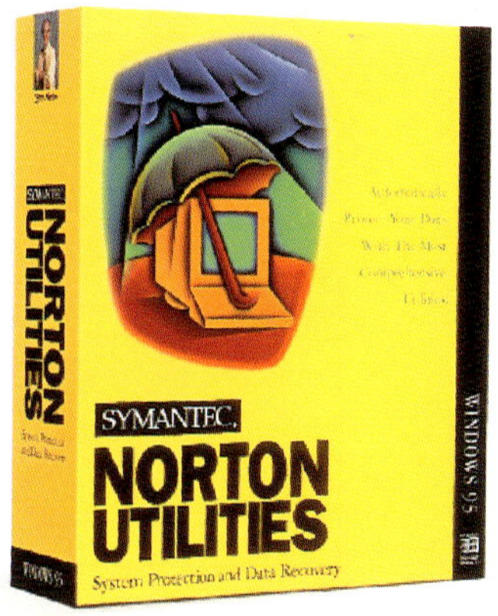

Radius, Inc.

What's the Radius of an Apple? The geometric formula may be inexact, but Radius Inc. has existed, figuratively, as a function of Apple Computer since its founding in 1986. It was started by Michael Boich and a few former Apple colleagues who worked on the original Macintosh. Its early mission was to build a superior color monitor for the Mac. Today Radius is run by another Apple alum, Charles W. Berger, under whose direction the company has blossomed

President Charles W. Berger is leading Radius into new fields

into a technology leader serving the needs of creative publishing and video professionals with large super resolution color displays, graphics accelerators, and digital video technology. And most recently the Radius/Apple connection came full circle when Apple licensed Radius to clone the Macintosh.

No other Apple seedling has grown more luxuriantly, particularly since the arrival of Berger as chairman, president, and chief executive officer in May 1993. Berger, a Pennsylvania native, emigrated to Silicon Valley in 1977 to join Memorex after a stint with a high-tech lending group at a Philadelphia bank. Then it was on to Apple for six years in the mid-1980s, leaving for an executive position at Sun Microsystems and then a senior vice presidency for worldwide sales at Claris, Apple's software subsidiary. Berger was then tapped to head up Radius.

The Radius Berger inherited had seen some turbulent management changes and was lagging its chief rival, SuperMac Technologies, in the color publishing arena.

Having grown too big for founder Boich to lead, Radius recruited a professional manager, Barry James Folsom, who headed the company until a rift with the Radius engineering team forced his departure.

Berger, one of Silicon Valley's younger CEOs, moved quickly to reorganize, refocus, and refinance the company. Under his leadership Radius soon passed SuperMac. Then in October 1994, Radius, as the acquiring company, merged with SuperMac and moved from San Jose to its former rival's Sunnyvale headquarters. The combined and much strengthened company swallowed most of the restructuring and acquisitions costs in a single financial quarter, showing three profitable quarters in FY1994.

Berger, however, still wasn't finished. Key to his strategic vision was positioning Radius so that it could emerge as a major player in the fast-growing digital media market. Radius had already captured the publishing market, by developing products that allowed these professionals to do their work on general-purpose Macintoshes at a fraction of the cost and difficulty of previous proprietary systems. Now he saw the same opportunity opening up in the rapidly expanding digital media world of video. This resulted in another key Radius acquisition: VideoFusion, Inc., a leading video effects and editing software applications company. Thus, by the end of 1994, Radius had moved into a key leadership position in both the color publishing and digital video worlds and was ready to launch a new generation of advanced products for the Power Macintosh.

Then Apple stunned the world and completely changed the rules of the game with its announcement that it would license the Macintosh Operating System (Mac™OS). Prior to that time, Apple had jealously guarded its OS, in part to protect what were once the lushest profit margins in the industry. In hindsight, many have seen this strategy as a mistake, in essence ceding the dominant market position to Microsoft, which had then what was generally recognized as an inferior operating system.

Although Radius was the second company to announce it had signed an agreement with Apple to license the Mac OS, it was the first company to unveil an actual working clone — at the MacWorld Expo trade show held in San Francisco in January 1995. In fact, it took Radius engineers all of three weeks to turn that feat, and therein lies another story.

Back a few years earlier, many of the 70 talented Radius engineers were engrossed in a project code-named "Skylab." They had secretly designed a hot-rod version of the Mac, with 12 microprocessors instead of the standard one. What they had, Berger realized, was the equivalent of a mini-supercomputer. But this "skunk works" operation had no authorization from Apple, and Berger, intent on focusing Radius, grounded the Skylab project. When Apple decided to change its strategy, Radius was ready—thanks to their experience with the Skylab skunk works and the legendary can-do attitude of Radius engineers.

In Berger's view, Radius' ability to clone a Macintosh CPU would give the company direct control over a key component of the hardware/software solutions they were now designing for color publishing and digital video professionals. Instead of having to adapt and work around the design of existing Macintosh systems, they could now design a Mac OS-based system to the exact specifications their high-end customers needed.

Radius customers are, to say the least, a demanding lot. Most are found within advertising agencies, corporate communications departments of large companies, graphic design firms, video production firms, printers, service bureaus, and multimedia companies. As creative professionals, they are always looking for new ways to improve the speed and functionality of their systems and to give them more raw horsepower to realize their creative ambitions. And the huge image and video files they work with are forever growing bigger, which in turn requires even faster systems to make manipulation of the files fast enough to be economical.

Radius has parlayed these needs into success before. Take their application-specific accelerators, which can reduce the computation times for specific tasks, like applying filters in Adobe Photoshop. Creative professionals using such Radius products can save up to 30 minutes a day of billable time — enough so that a typical design firm can recoup its investment in a matter of weeks. Or take Radius' digital video products, which have allowed independent producers and broadcast designers to capture, composite, add effects, and produce high-quality video at a fraction of the time and cost of traditional technologies like editing studios.

Finally, there are game developers and corporate multimedia professionals who rely on Radius video products and Cinepak compression technology to produce and compress digital video for use on CD-ROMs, over the World Wide Web, and for training and presentation applications.

Now, with the shipment of the first Radius personal computer workstation, the Radius System 100, in March of 1995, all the pieces of CEO Berger's grand design are in place.

What does the future have in store for Radius? As readers of leading newspapers and magazines know, color publishing is growing fast. Even more dramatic growth may lie ahead; the percentage of publishing done in color is forecast to go up from 30% today to 70% by 1997! Looked at another way, the color publishing market is expected to grow 30% a year through 1997, while the digital video market expands by 25% each year. Macintosh sales, too, are expected to grow quickly. With a leadership position firmly established in these markets, Radius is positioned like no one else to take advantage of this phenomenal growth. And if past accomplishments are any guide, the public can expect to see the company stay right on the leading edge of technology and continue to pioneer new and better ways to serve tomorrow's professionals in the 21st century.

Co-founder Michael Boich led Radius in developing a superior color monitor for the Macintosh

Finis F. Conner, co-founder and chief executive of Conner Peripherals

Rocketing from obscurity to Fortune 500 fame and fortune in its first three years of operation, Conner Peripherals, Inc., has been one of the major movers and shakers of the disk drive industry since its inception in 1986. Propelled by a team of seasoned industry veterans (a rarity in itself), this San Jose, California-based company had swollen by 1989 to $705 million in revenue and 5,000 employees, the fastest-growing manufacturing start-up in U.S. business history.

Leading the team then, as now, was Finis F. Conner, the flamboyant innovator, cofounder, chairman, and CEO of Conner Peripherals. Previously, Conner cofounded disk-drive makers Shugart Associates in 1973 and Seagate Technology in 1979.

The combined experience of Conner's seasoned executive team, coupled with an uncanny ability to anticipate market need and bring product to market with astonishing speed, fueled the company's rapid ascent. When 5.25-inch drives were still the standard by which computers read, wrote, and stored data, Conner foresaw the forthcoming switch to 3.5-inch drives — and capitalized on it.

Not only did the company possess the vision and the technological capability to bring that vision to fruition, Conner also adopted a unique and some may say, risky, strategy. Unlike other firms that developed the technology and then set out to sell it, Conner sold the concept, then designed and built the products around the customer's specifications. One early customer who took full advantage of this approach was Compaq Computer Corp., one of today's leading PC manufacturers. For example, rather than adapt an existing 3.5-inch Conner drive for a notebook computer Compaq was developing, Conner accommodated Compaq's request for a super-thin 3.5-inch drive.

Of course, many other OEMs — virtually every major computer system manufacturer in America, Asia, and Europe — have been or are Conner customers. In 1990, sales topped $1.34 billion, and Conner became the first manufacturing company to earn more than $1 billion in revenues after four years of operation.

Two years ago, faced with increasing competition, a rapidly and dramatically changing computer industry, and cut-throat price wars, Conner took a daring but necessary leap into the future. In 1992, Conner began the sometimes painful transformation from major manufacturer solely of Winchester disk drives for personal computers and workstations into a leading supplier of total storage solutions for the computer industry. Conner began by acquiring Archive Corporation, a leading supplier of tape drives, storage systems, and storage management software. Then, in 1994, Conner formed Arcada Software, Inc., by combining the software operations it acquired from Archive with those of Quest Development Corp., a privately held data manage-

Conner's Singapore plant is one of the most advanced facilities of its kind

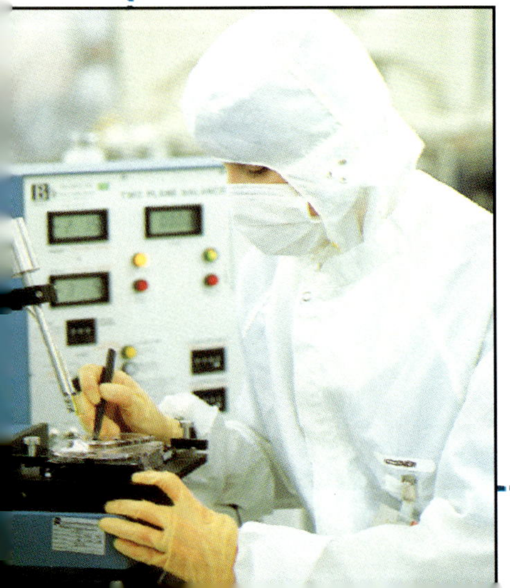

Conner disk drives are assembled in sophisticated clean rooms in Asia, Europe and the U.S.

Conner is a technology leader in an industry that increases storage capacity 60% a year—for the same price!

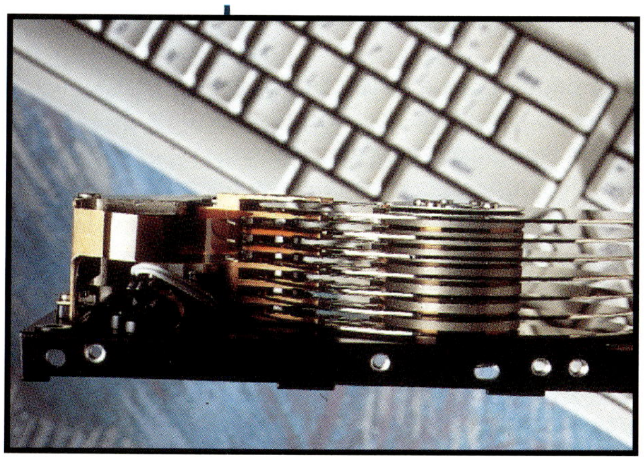

ment software developer. Today, Arcada comprises one of the largest data management software teams in the industry.

This transition did not come without cost. In 1993, Conner faced the most challenging year in its history. With sales of $2.2 billion, the company reported a net loss of $445 million, due in large part to a write-down associated with the acquisition of Archive and the introduction of 30 new products, four times that of any previous period. That same year, the company restructured, slimmed down, and tightened up, returning to profitability by the fourth quarter. During 1994, Conner earned $109.7 million on revenues of $2.4 billion.

Conner produces most of its disk drives, tape drives, and storage systems by purchasing subassemblies and key components and configuring them into finished products. The company's worldwide operations occupy more than 1.5 million square feet, with R&D facilities in Colorado, Florida, and California, and manufacturing sites in Colorado, California, Singapore, Malaysia, Italy, and the People's Republic of China (another industry first). Conner also operates nine U.S. sales offices and eight international sales offices, as well as a manufacturing partnership in Japan.

Conner entered 1995 with a wide range of new products providing the full array of storage options for virtually every application — from entry-level personal computers to high-performance networks. The company employs a trademark "Sell, Design, Build" strategy of listening to customers' needs first, then designing and building products accordingly.

In September 1995, Conner and Seagate Technology Inc. announced that they were negotiating a merger valued at $1.1 billion. If approved, the merger of No. 2 Seagate and No. 3 Conner would create America's largest computer storage company with revenues in excess of $7.5 billion and about a third of the computer disk drives market.

Finis Conner and Al Shugart of Seagate have been both teammates and rivals. They cofounded both Shugart Associates and Seagate, but parted ways when Conner left to start his own company. Seagate is based in Scotts Valley, California. Whatever the fate of the proposed merger, the impact of Conner Peripherals on computer storage history will remain indelible.

2.5-inch hard drive is slightly larger than a credit card

Minicartridge tape drive is one of Conner Peripherals' data protection products

Frame Technology

L. George Klaus, Frame Technology president and chief executive officer

Back in 1986, when Frame Technology Corporation was founded, people who had to prepare and share documents electronically cussed and muttered a lot. Not only were there many limitations to what they could do in writing and editing documents, but incompatibility was a huge problem if they had exchange documents with places using different computer systems.

Frame Technology was determined to overcome all that. And it has. Today the company provides document-based information management solutions for worldwide markets. These solutions encompass the authoring, management, and distribution of business and technical documents across multiple computing platforms. For example, today Frame enables customers such as the European Space Agency to distribute complex documents–documents with graphics and intricate typesetting–across a mixed network of systems including PCs using Windows, Apple Macintoshes or Power Macintoshes, and all leading UNIX workstations.

Frame's flagship product, FrameMaker, now in version 5, automates common publishing tasks. It numbers chapters, footnotes, and illustrations, and keeps the numbers up to date. FrameMaker creates cross-references within and between documents; checks for mistakes such as repeated words, extra spaces, and other typographical errors; and easily imports text and graphics from popular word processing and illustration packages. It wraps text around various shapes as if that were no trick at all.

FrameMaker, the firm's flagship product: automates common publishing tasks

FrameMaker also makes the almost certain last-minute changes a breeze.

FrameMaker is part of a broad family of Frame Technology products designed to help organizations get the most out of their documents. Other products include FrameViewer, FrameMaker+SGML (Standard Generalized Markup Language), and Document Management. The company's products range from off-the-shelf software to customized, corporatewide solutions for giant global companies.

More than 450,000 people worldwide use Frame's family of software solutions. In addition to supporting SGML, the leading international document exchange standard, Frame products support HyperText Markup Language for publishing on the Internet. Internet users can access Frame's World Wide Web documents at http://www.frame.com.

The company is headquartered in downtown San Jose, California, across the street from a tower Adobe Systems plans to occupy. In June 1995, Adobe Systems moved to acquire Frame for about $500 million in stock–a step requiring approval by Frame stockholders in September 1995.

The merger promises to create one of the largest independent software companies. Adobe CEO John Warnock said the goal of the merger is to forge a unit that can scale new heights in electronic publishing, such as supplying software technology that enables people to create electronic versions of newspapers and magazines. Frame and Adobe had made a commitment to make their software products work together seamlessly, signaled by a pact to provide hassle-free font handling and sharing for UNIX-based applications. The new FrameMaker release incorporates advanced support for Adobe Acrobat.

Frame Technology is a publicly traded corporation (NASDAQ:FRAM). It has Canadian headquarters in Markham, Ontario, and European headquarters in London. Frame also has offices in Japan, France, Germany, and the Netherlands..

L. George Klaus is Frame's president and chief executive officer, and Thomas F. Kelly is its executive vice president and chief financial officer. One of the company's four founders, Charles Corfield, remains active as chief technical officer.

In the past decade, Frame Technology has done a lot to advance the art of electronic document preparation and sharing. The company's achievements figure to be perpetuated far into the future.

Running text around an irregular shape, such as a photo of a telephone, is easily done with Frame Technology software

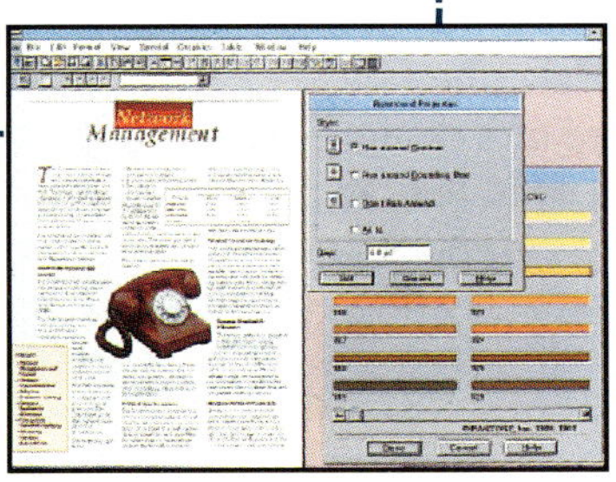

Andy Ludwick, who formerly headed SynOptics, is CEO of Bay Networks

On one end of the information superhighway lie the computer systems; at the other lie the carrier services. In between, connecting and interfacing the other two components, lies the network. At the core of the network is a managed, high-speed communications system. Bay Networks is a leading supplier of networking communications systems — and the newborn prodigal son of two industry leaders — WellFleet Communications, Inc. and SynOptics Communications, Inc.

Founded in 1986, WellFleet provides high-performance information internetworking products and related services. A *Fortune* 500 company founded in 1985, SynOptics supplies intelligent hub, high-speed switching systems, and sophisticated network management software. The two companies merged in 1994 to form Bay Networks, creating a $1 billion company that now dominates the new switched internetworking market.

The networking environment has changed radically since SynOptics was first established in Santa Clara, California, in 1985. SynOptics has invested heavily in R&D to champion this new frontier. In 1987, SynOptics pioneered the technology to run Ethernet over unshielded twisted pair (UTP) wiring, resulting in the 10BASE-T standard — the most prevalent LAN connectivity method used today.

Since 1989, SynOptics has driven the development of FDDI technology. In 1991, SynOptics teamed up with IBM to develop technology to allow 16 Mb/s Token Ring to run on Category 3 UTP wiring. In 1993, the company introduced its first ATM products, providing a commercially viable product with a form factor and price point unparalleled in the industry.

SynOptics has also delivered significant advances in network management., including its early Lattis® and current Optivity® families of network management software systems. In 1993, SynOptics worked with major industry partners to develop the first global enterprise management applications, which unify and automate the management desktop systems and WAN equipment, as well as the network "fabric."

The merged company of SynOptics and WellFleet represents the single largest merger in the history of the networking industry, combining two of the fastest-growing companies in the United States. The new company — Bay Networks — markets and manufactures a comprehensive line of networking products and services, including high-speed routers, wide area network access devices, local area network switches, intelligent hubs, network management software, as well as network design and configuration services.

The former SynOptics building in Santa Clara now is the headquarters and western base of Bay Networks

Bay Networks employs 3,000 employees in 110 offices worldwide. Corporate headquarters and western operations are located in the previous SynOptics facilities near Great America in Santa Clara. Eastern operations are located at the previous WellFleet facilities in Billerica, Massachusetts. The name Bay Networks represents both the San Francisco Bay Area, which is home to SynOptics, and the "Bay State" of Massachusetts, home to WellFleet. It also highlights the networking expertise of both firms.

Bay Networks has also established key alliance partnerships with industry leaders such as AT&T, Apple, Hewlett-Packard, IBM, Intel, MCI, Network General, Novell, Sprint, StrataCom, Sun Microsystems, and WilTel. With these partnerships and the combined, focused strengths of its parent companies, Bay Networks is well positioned to pave the way in networking technology of the 21st century.

Paul Severino, chairman of the board, Bay Networks

Leaders, from left, include founder Janusz Bryzek, former president Derek Bell, founder Joe Mallon, and founder Kurt Petersen

Silicon is strictly an electronics material, right? Wrong! Mechanical devices can be made from it, too, by the emerging technology called micromachining. Micromachining employs three-dimensional sculpting of silicon, fabricating thousands of devices on a single wafer in a batch mode identical to that used to manufacture integrated circuits. This approach yields low-cost mechanical microstructures with dimensions smaller than a human hair—devices used in automotive pressure sensors, blood pressure measuring devices, and in a broad range of consumer and industrial pressure sensor applications.

Why silicon? It is mechanically stable; as strong as steel, but three times lighter; and highly sensitive to stress and temperature. And it allows silicon micromachinists to enjoy all the miracle technologies of the huge electronics industry.

NovaSensor was founded in 1985 by three pioneers of micromachining technology: Dr. Janusz Bryzek, Joseph R. Mallon Jr., and Dr. Kurt Petersen. Their vision was to manufacture advanced micromachined sensors and microstructures, beginning with pressure sensors. Their strategy was to create a team and develop sensor solutions that bridged the gap between those using traditional silicon sensor technologies (dating back to early diodes and transistors) and technologies being explored in academic circles. In the process, NovaSensor created widespread awareness of the emerging microelectromechanical systems (MEMS) industry.

Bryzek began his silicon sensor career in Poland while completing his doctorate in electrical engineering. After several years with Honeywell's sensor group, he joined IC Transducers, the first sensor spin-off company from Fairchild Semiconductor. In 1981 he developed the first low-cost, disposable blood pressure sensor, a device with current annual sales of nearly 20 million units. Later he cofounded two other sensor companies: Sensym and ICSensors.

Mallon joined the world's first silicon sensor company, Kulite Semiconductor, in 1965. Kulite initially commercialized the silicon piezoresistivity discovered at Bell Laboratories. Mallon pioneered many technological "firsts" and actively developed markets, creating a foundation for today's micromachining.

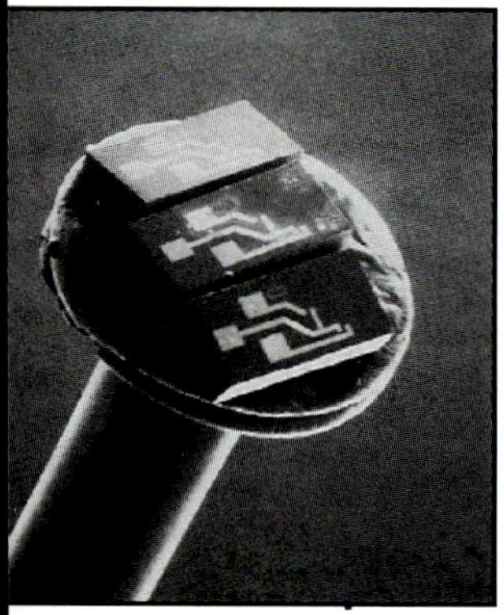

Magnified photo shows three medical sensors on the head of a pin

Petersen, who earned his doctorate in electrical engineering at MIT, worked for IBM Research from 1975-1982. Assigned to develop state-of-the-art mechanical ICs, he pioneered many advanced silicon microstructures and developed several micromachining processes. His 1982 IEEE Proceedings paper, "Silicon as a Mechanical Material"—micromachining's manifesto—brought Petersen unofficial renown as "the father of micromachining." He cofounded a Silicon Valley R&D start-up, Transensory Devices, in 1982.

Five months after its founding, in October 1985, NovaSensor was awarded a $1.1 million order for a new generation of disposable blood pressure sensors. The company had only seven people, a 1000 square-foot office, no wafer fab, no equipment, and no design! Despite these hurdles, NovaSensor delivered the order ahead of schedule. Meanwhile, the founders designed a custom facility in Fremont. The 28,000 square-foot headquarters, occupied in 1986, accommodates offices, assembly areas, and clean rooms.

Original equity funding for NovaSensor came from Schlumberger. During its first four years, the company invested heavily in R&D. In 1990, NovaSensor negotiated an acquisition by Lucas, a $4 billion British corporation.

One major NovaSensor breakthrough was commercialization of silicon fusion bonding—welding two or more silicon wafers together. This enabled high-volume, low-cost production, benefitting several products, including the smallest commercial pressure sensor. This chip (smaller than a poppy seed) is mounted on a catheter for insertion into the human heart to measure blood pressure. Silicon fusion bonding also enabled space shuttle pressure sensors to operate during hot re-entries.

NovaSensor finished fiscal 1995 with over 150 employees and sales of approximately $20 million. New markets for micromachined devices are opening in such areas as microfluidics, displays, memory storage, genetic engineering, and inertial navigation. Look for Lucas NovaSensor in micromachining's forefront.

Lucas NovaSensor headquarters in Fremont

CKS founders (from left) Bill Cle
and Tom Suitor in the control ro

In less than a decade CKS Group has mushroomed as Silicon Valley's largest advertising and integrated marketing agency, en route redefining the way advanced technology is used to produce marketing communications services.

Bill Cleary, the "C" in CKS, began the enterprise in 1987 and was joined by cofounders Mark Kvamme in 1989 and Tom Suiter in 1991. All three cut their marketing teeth at Apple Computer.

In a 22,000 square foot former Apple TV facility in Cupertino, California, CKS Pictures, Inc., in 1994 opened a broadcast and video production facility.Video equipment in the facility is used to create new marketing options on the information superhighway, from infomercials, television shows, and home shopping to multimedia, CD-ROM, and interactive TV services.

CKS headquarters, originally in nearby Campbell, moved to the Cupertino facility. CKS offices in Cupertino, Campbell, San Francisco, Portland, Oregon, and London, England, are linked on a high-speed optical fiber network.

CKS Group comprises three units: CKS Pictures, CKS Interactive, and CKS Partners. Besides its technological savvy, the group provides expertise in marketing strategy, advertising, corporate identity, packaging, sales promotion, direct marketing, and multimedia. All of the partners have had careers on the client side, the usual place for integrating marketing disciplines. CKS Interactive designs such things as the user interface for HP and interactive CDs and demo disks for trade show presentations, as well as Internet sites such as The Tonight Show for NBC. CKS Partners handles more traditional advertising and marcom work.

The segmented setup has helped the group land special orders from companies that retain major advertising agencies. Its expertise in new media and online services drove a strategic alliance with Interpublic Group, a global advertising-

Antennas send and receive real-time traffic between CKS offices and satellite networks

agency holding co
CKS's technology.
Rivals have dis
Valley rating on gr
based advertising
al capitalized billin
Kvamme (say Kwa
"Advertising agenc
in the communicat
advertising busine
will face the same
turers did at the tu
Senior Partner
one-stop shop noti
ing CKS: "Our rec
gence of media m
form; our philosop
ing communicatio
computers to come
ative solutions."
Suiter serves
in Cupertino. He h
specialty at Lando
CKS.
One CKS crea
attention is its
Electronic Job Jac
computer program
tracking all produ
costs on each proj
allows CKS to wor
more efficiently a
cost effectively, w
maintaining high
ative standards.
On most crea
teams, CKS adds
grammer to the us
copywriter-art dir
annual investment
hardware and soft
Kvamme beli
speed delivery of
ation-production t
50-50 to 90-10. He
ments return $30
ee–about three ti
Major clients
McDonald's, Nati
Computer. CKS r
million; Kvamme
record year for th
range.

1995 computer graphics calendar art shows a rainbow hitting a chambered nautilus rising from the sea on a pedestal

The business known today as ASCI–Art and Science of Computer Imaging–has operated since 1959 at the same address in Los Altos, California, but has changed radically since Manuel (Max) Freedman took it over in 1986.

Freedman graduated from Stanford in 1966, with credentials rare for a high-technology professional: a playwrighting scholarship in drama, with a minor in art history. His lifelong goal of writing and directing feature films accounts for ASCI being a computer-movie and computer-publications company today.

The predecessor business published newsletters and handled office tasks for independent executives and local firms. Freedman overlaid these activities with the marketing consulting practice he brought aboard.

Initially, all design and documentation work was word-processed on an IBM PC. Composition work was painstakingly pasted up at a light table.

The spark for today's business was kindled with the purchase of an Apple Macintosh in 1987. As ASCI's skills and technology inventory grew, output rose to ever-higher standards. By 1995, the studio's reputation for excellence had spread to clientele across the United States and in Canada, England, and other countries. ASCI won renown for meeting exceedingly tight deadlines for major projects while maintaining superior quality standards.

On March 30, 1989, the name was changed to ASCI–A Service for Creative Ideas. Next, the company solidified its commitment to high-end computer graphics by purchasing a Silicon Graphics computer system and Wavefront Technologies 3-D animation software. Then, on October 17, the Loma Prieta earthquake shook the dozen employees and clients in ASCI's two office suites. The quake disruption was made much worse a month later when burglars stole two whole Macintosh publishing systems. More than aftershocks rattled personnel through the holidays, capping a year of tumultuous changes.

In 1990, the 3-D studio released its first full computer-generated animation, while the publications group rose to prominence with clients like Acuson Corporation and Apple Computer. Acuson user manuals published by ASCI won awards for excellence in 1992-93 against 30 rival entries. Late in 1992, ASCI sent as holiday greetings the first in a series of spectacular 3-D computer graphics calendars; requests for new works have mushroomed yearly since then.

Producing corporate videos for trade shows and training has helped the company grow. The creative team writes, produces, and directs these from a feature-film perspective, building the high production values audiences expect from first-run theatrical films and network broadcasts.

In 1994, Silicon Graphics retained ASCI to create a 30-second animated commercial to be played on CD-ROMs. A breakthrough in video compression, it allowed playback of the animation at full speed and size with stereo sound directly from the CD-ROM, without hardware or software adjustments. Silicon Graphics then added it as a signature piece to its other corporate video productions.

By 1994, the interpretation of the acronym ASCI no longer fit. It was changed to Art and Science of Computer Imaging, describing the company more accurately.

Today, ASCI is a digital entertainment and educational publications production studio. It produces 3-D animations, digital movies, special effects and images for feature films, TV commercials, magazine ads, CD-ROMs, games, corporate videos, tradeshows, museum displays, theme parks, World Wide Web pages, kiosks, and disk- and print-based presentations. The company strives to create beautiful image compositions and stunning movies for consumers in every audio-visual medium.

The company's own poster displays full-color, three dimensional computer graphics design skills

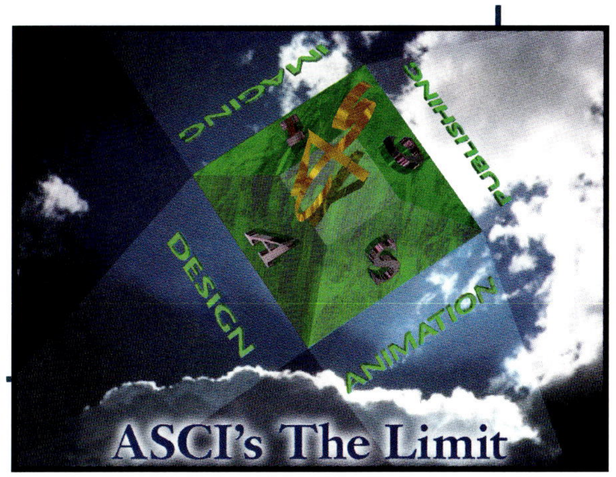

Target Therapeutics

Target Therapeutics was created in 1985 as a joint venture between Collagen Corporation of Palo Alto and Advanced Cardiovascular Systems (ACS), a subsidiary of Eli Lilly & Co. A group of Collagen researchers teamed up with ACS catheter engineers. The goal was not only to deliver anti-cancer agents directly to the site of a tumor but also to block the tumor's blood supply, thereby "starving" it. The result was a breakthrough in medical devices.

In 1986 a catheter called the Tracker® was developed. It was able to navigate through very narrow, sharply turning vasculature and reach previously inaccessible areas of the body. "Variable stiffness" was the key to the development of this valuable new tool. The tubing was soft enough to bend through tortuous vasculature, but strong enough to be pushed along a guidewire through narrow, winding vessels where blood flow alone was inadequate to carry the catheter forward.

Introduced in 1987, a variable stiffness catheter/guidewire combination was the first technology to provide ready access to small vessels in the periphery of the body and in the brain. In the same year, ACS sold its interest in Target to Collagen, which holds an approximate 33% equity position.

Other firms also were developing catheter-based technologies, but Target's was unique in its ongoing focus on access to small blood vessels in the brain. (Coronary branch vessels are very tiny, approximating 2-4 millimeters.) It gave physicians their first opportunity to reach quickly and safely through the vessels at the base of the skull and into the vessels of the brain. This made possible new therapeutic approaches to neurological conditions previously treatable only by surgery.

Using Target catheters, neuroradiologists can now deliver clot-dissolving drugs directly on a blockage in the brain, accurately insert a stabilizing coil into an aneurysm, or dilate narrowed arteries with an angioplasty balloon.

From the outset, Target's product development has been carried on in collaboration with physician customers, yielding a variety of highly innovative products. The Seeker guidewire, for example, was originally created in conjunction with University of Wisconsin physicians. Target's

first microcoils for
tions in the brain w
done by several co
California, San Fra
A new microco
ideas of Dr. Guido
neurosurgeon and
gist. The Guglielm
which had been in
markets for some t
tests and was certi
Administration in S
designed to treat a
suboptimal candid
In fiscal 1995,
$47.5 million, more
seas, with research
of 22% of revenues
300 employees, no
nies. Conceptus, C
are developing inn
ways to treat infer
damaged blood ve
In 1992, Targe
(NASDAQ:TGET)
new headquarters
Although Targ
refined during the
President and Chi
Bang says, "We kr
in interventional m
ahead."

Gary
big a

A Target Tracker
perimeter of a pa

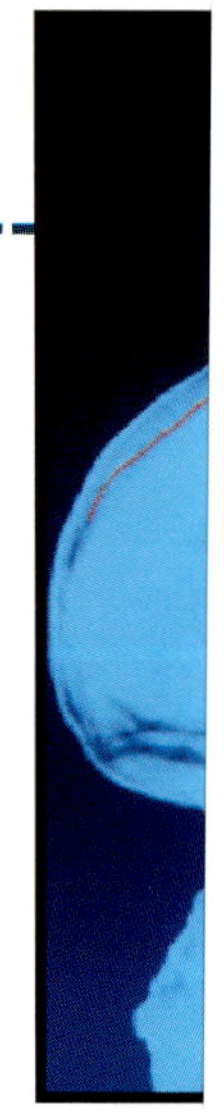

S3 Incorporated

S3 personnel create the first single chip Graphical User Interface accelerator in 1991

For "baby boomers" coming of age in the '60s, '70s, and '80s, Silicon Valley was the place to be. They came from near and far, seeking golden opportunities in the promising new land of high technology. Some, like S3 Incorporated founders Diosdado (Dado) Banatao and Ronald Yara, came to *create* that opportunity.

Yara, a native of Hawaii, moved to the San Francisco Bay Area after receiving an electrical engineering degree from Purdue University and working for a short time with McDonnell Douglas, St. Louis, Missouri. He immediately put his technical degree to work at DataPathing in Sunnyvale. Then, he changed career directions, holding product marketing positions with Raytheon Semiconductor, Scientific Micro Systems, and Intel. Along the way, he earned a master's degree in electrical engineering from Santa Clara University.

Banatao earned his undergraduate electrical engineering degree from the Mapua Institute of Technology in his native land, the Philippines, then master's degrees in electrical engineering and computer science from Stanford University. He cut his teeth on senior engineering management jobs with several Silicon Valley companies, including Seeq Technology and National Semiconductor.

Banatao teamed up with Yara to form S3 in January 1989, determined to make their third start-up even more successful than the two previous ones. Earlier, they had been in on the founding of a motherboard maker and a chip-set developer. Initially, they set out at S3 to build a lightning-fast PC. Venture capitalists, however, advised them to concentrate on what they knew best: graphics acceleration. They did.

S3 accelerator cards enhance performance of personal computers in processing graphics

Five years later, S3, located in Santa Clara, California, claimed 25% of what is now a $450 million global market—with 40% profit margins. In 1993, S3 made its initial public offering, and its revenues reached $113 million. By 1994, S3 revenues totaled $140 million. Analysts predicted revenues above $250 million for 1995, a forecast borne out by revenues totaling $128 million in the first two quarters.

Anticipating the explosive growth of such graphics-heavy operating systems as Microsoft Windows and IBM's OS/2, S3 created the world's first single-chip Graphical User Interface (GUI) accelerator in 1991. S3's products relieve PCs from the burden of processing graphics, significantly enhancing system performance. In 1992, S3 became the first graphics accelerator company to have its driver shipped with Microsoft Video for Windows and the only one to have a driver included with the beta release of Microsoft Windows NT. The company's unique design approach — from the system down, rather than from the chip up — has resulted in the selection of the S3 architecture by a growing number of leading PC manufacturers, such as Compaq, Dell, Digital, Hewlett-Packard, and IBM.

Under the leadership of industry veterans Banatao (chairman), Yara (senior vice president of strategic marketing), and President/CEO Terry N. Holdt, who joined the firm in 1992, S3 continues to create exciting opportunities in graphics accelerator technology. Today, S3's product line is gaining momentum as the number one choice for a wide range of next-generation PC products. And S3's leaders have become an inspiration to a whole new generation coming of age in the information/communications revolution.

A number of leading PC makers have chosen the S3 architecture

Robert Madge, Chairman and CEO, directly in front of tree, with colleagues in 1986

Madge Networks is a leading, worldwide supplier of local area network (LAN) solutions for businesses–typically large corporations in the global *Fortune* 1,000 ranks. The company is recognized throughout the networking industry for its technology leadership and commitment to customer support without limits.

Madge Networks began in 1986, when its founder and chief executive officer, Robert Madge, mortgaged his farm in Buckinghamshire, England, to pursue his dream of building a global networking company. That dream is now realized with Madge Networks.

Madge Networks specializes in the multipurpose, high-bandwidth networks of the future, notably Token Ring and Ethernet switching and Asynchronous Transfer Mode (ATM) networking products. ATM is a type of switching technology in which the switches are small, fixed-length cells containing data.

In addition to the farmhouse, where training continues today, the company has four major business centers around the world, located in San Jose, California; London; Hong Kong; and Tokyo. Madge serves its multinational customers from 40 locations worldwide.

In San Jose, the heart of Silicon Valley, the company has experienced phenomenal growth. In 1991, Madge Networks had 12 full-time employees in its San Jose office. As of mid-1995, there were 200, with hiring and expansion continuing.

Madge conducts research and development, finance, marketing, manufacturing, and general operations from San Jose, where Marc Jones is the group president and chief operating officer. Of the company's record $213.3 million in revenue in 1994, the U.S. operations generated 46%. Since the company shipped its first product in 1987, Madge has become a leading supplier of Token Ring networking hardware and software, and is second only to IBM in worldwide Token Ring adapter card shipments.

Today, Madge's mission statement is "Switching to ATM." The company provides products and services to integrate today's local area networks with the emerging network technology, ATM. Madge plays a key role in defining standards for ATM and is an active member of the ATM Forum and the Desktop ATM25 Alliance. In addition, it sponsors the *Madge ATM News Digest*.

From the licensing of its Token Ring protocol stack to Microsoft in 1988 to the introduction of Fastmac Plus in 1993, Madge has been a leader in providing technologically superior Token Ring products.

Since 1986, Madge has been at the forefront of Token Ring technology, with a series of industry firsts:

- First to download multiple LAN products to the adapter card.
- First to provide full utilization of Token Ring bandwidth.
- First to optimize full bandwidth of modern PC buses.
- First to offer IBM plug-compatible stackable hub.
- First to license Token Ring core technology.

The company's devotion to quality has been recognized by the Queen's Award for Exports in Great Britain, and by the International Standards Organization's ISO 9002 certification for quality management in manufacturing. In addition, Madge's technology leadership has been recognized by the industry and has recently garnered these awards:

Smart 16/4 EISA Ringnode—Editor's Choice, *PC Magazine*, October 1992; The Best of Times, *LAN Times*, December 1993; Best Token Ring NIC, *Network Computing*, April 1995.

Smart 100 EISA Ringnode—Tester's Choice, *Data Communications*, July 1994; Product of the Year, *LAN Magazine,* February 1994.

With its superior family of products and services, and its continued investment in ATM and other future networking technologies, Madge Networks is well on its way to realizing its mission to become the world's number one switched networking vendor for large enterprises.

Madge Networks started in 1986 at this farmhouse in Buckinghamshire, England

Ropers, Majeski, Kohn & Bentley conducts a multiservice practice offering litigation and transactional services in the areas of corporate law, banking, financial institutions, intellectual property, real estate, environmental law, estate planning, health care, regulatory matters, and appellate practice.

Harold Ropers and Eugene J. Majeski established the firm in Redwood City in 1950. Initially they specialized in insurance defense work. As the firm has grown, the scope of services it offers has expanded. With over 180 attorneys in six offices — Los Angeles, San Francisco, San Jose, Redwood City, Santa Rosa, and Sacramento, and an affiliating office in Hong Kong — Ropers, Majeski remains committed to providing its clients with comprehensive services in a cost-effective manner. Over the past 40 years, the firm has become one of the most experienced and successful civil and commercial litigation firms in California.

Eleven partners have been admitted to the prestigious American Board of Trial Advocates, and in 1989, the board selected founding partner Majeski as its "Trial Lawyer of the Year."

Ropers, Majeski has grown in response to the needs of its expanding business clientele. The sophistication of current entrepreneurial and business practices is reflected in the firm's many specialized lawyers. The list includes developing managed health care institutions, capitation contracting, and health care reform; assisting financial institutions in mergers, acquisitions, loan workouts, and other problems; and intellectual property and patent litigation in the state and federal courts.

In some complex litigation, traditional legal approaches are frequently too time consuming and costly. Ropers, Majeski brings to the table a business approach to problem solving. There is probably no firm in California with a greater depth of experienced trial lawyers and they have used those abilities to great advantage in successful arbitration and mediation of disputes.

The Thrill of Discovery

"We started making pictures that were so photorealistic that we couldn't believe that we had done it in a way with non-impact printing, which was what the whole field was called, inkjet being only one part of it. And I guess the most exciting part of the project, once we made the pictures, we started making many pictures, and reproduction quality was beyond our imagination. I knew we had done something. We weren't sure of the impact."

—Annette Jaffe
Developer of color inkjet technology

"One of the advances was the ear implant which is a spin-off from the micromachining group at Stanford. This is a thin plastic needle that has a bunch of electrodes on it and you insert it in the ear in a deaf person and you can excite the nerves in the ear electrically through this little array of probes and you can actually restore hearing. They do this in some children now; you can restore hearing in totally deaf children and it's just a fantastic advance."

—Kurt Petersen
Father of micromachining

"I recently heard a lecture which was recounting the history of the main disease that our laser treated, which was the condition known as diabetic retinopathy, and the statistics are that in 1966, if you contracted diabetic retinopathy, there was a 50 percent chance that you would be blind within 10 years. Today that chance has been reduced to one percent. So we're very proud of the contribution."

—*James Hobart*
founder & CEO, Coherent, Inc.

"Engineers are all identified with their own product. And they all have a desire to get their product out and they want it to be the best product of that type in the world. And there's a lot of other engineers looking over their shoulder or they ask questions within the group because any idea that's a good idea that they can incorporate into their product makes it a better product and they're happy to do it because the identity of it is still with them."

—*Robert C. Dobkin*
analog engineer
founder, Linear Technology

"I think it was toward the end of 1975, there was some discussion in a number of scientific journals on the potential of recombinant DNA technology to produce useful products, and I got very excited about the potential of the technology and I started calling up scientists in different parts of the country at different universities because the science was all within the academic world at that point. One of the early people I called was Dr. Herbert Boyer at the University of California, and he was the only one I called who agreed with me at the time and thought that this science not only had potential, but something could be done immediately. There would be a way to make a useful product today, and he was a cold call. I'd never met him before.... It turned out that he was clearly one of the leaders in the whole field. I tried to convince him to see me, and he was very polite and nice, but he said that he was awfully busy. I said, 'No, you don't understand. You're the only one I've talked to that thinks something can be done now.' Finally he relented and said, well, ten minutes on Friday afternoon. So I showed up at his lab at U.C. San Francisco, in my suit, and everybody else was in jeans and T-shirts, and we hit it off. It turned into three or four hours and about that many beers. We found out that not only did we like each other, but we shared a common vision, and from that point, I went about putting together a business plan. This was January of 1976. Herb helped put together some of the technical aspects of the business plan, and we each put in our $500 and incorporated Genentech in 19, on April 7, 1976.... What we were proposing to do in 1976 and that had never been done before was to take a human gene and put it into a microorganism with the correct coding sequence, make a lot of whatever follows, and in this case, human insulin for treating diabetes. And so it was the first time that anybody succeeded in producing a human hormone or really any product in the microorganism. That was what was so exciting and that happened a little over a year after we got started. That was in late summer of 1977."

—*Robert A. Swanson*
founder, Genentech

1991

U.S.-led allies liberate Kuwait in 100 hours.

Lithuanian voters overwhelmingly back independence.

Rajiv Gandhi assassinated in India.

Strategic Arms Reduction Treaty signed at Moscow summit.

Soviet President Mikhail Gorbachev survived a coup attempt.

United Nations welcomes seven new members, including North and South Korea.

Islamic Jihad releases Terry Anderson, U.S. newsman held for 2,455 days.

Chapter 16: Morphing, Downsizing, and Restructuring

Terminator 2: Judgment Day, 1991's hit movie, opened the public's eyes to a new era of digital imaging and special effects that was being born in Silicon Valley and the regional multimedia community. Through morphing, a technique employed by George Lucas' Industrial Light and Magic company, the film's "bad guy" came out of the floor and changed shapes at will. Although the digitizing behind morphing took costly special computer equipment to accomplish, the era it introduced was to lead to CD-ROMs on many home computers and inexpensive programs for putting photos on disk and manipulating them.

Progress and pain both marked the Valley's 1991-92 period. Total jobs in Santa Clara County declined by 25,000 as defense companies downsized and large high-technology companies restructured. However, real wages, exports, and venture capital all gained. The U.S. pulled even with Japan in semiconductor sales in 1992—a prelude to forging ahead.

Silicon Valley ranked as a global leader in integrated circuits, microprocessors, personal computers, CD-ROMs, networking, and three-dimensional imaging. Software became the region's fastest-growing job generator.

The Valley also mulled a new initiative—the idea of creating a Joint Venture: Silicon Valley Network that would function as a coordinating body to bring together industry and civic figures to make the area more receptive to industries' needs and more collaborative in meeting its governmental needs.

SLAC's 2-mile "gun"

In 1991, several companies introduced wireless local area network systems (LANs). Using nondirectional microwave technology, unlike old systems that had to be beamed at a specific target, LANs could handle data transmission speeds similar to those used for existing wire installations.

A trend was running toward lightweight notebook computers, including 5-pound laptops such as Apple's model. Although the year was turbulent, the computer industry recession appeared to have ended.

AT&T divested itself of 19 million shares of Sun Microsystems Inc. stock at a profit exceeding $200 million. The move was related to AT&T's hostile takeover of NCR Corporation, which became its networked computing resource.

The Soviet Union and its Communist Party collapsed completely in 1991, alleviating fears that a crisis might somehow bring on nuclear warfare. But in a new "post-Cold War" era, no one could clearly see what was coming. In the Persian Gulf, a U.S.-led coalition of countries gave Iran a stunning "high tech" defeat after Iran invaded and annexed Kuwait.

In 1992, a court decision opened the way for "Baby Bells" (regional telephone operating systems once part of AT&T) to offer home computer users electronic Yellow Pages in the short run and, later, on-line interactive video. This step was one of a number leading to the often-predicted convergence of computers, telecommunications, and cable TV. Industry analysts foresaw each field competing for the others' customers.

Novelties on the '92 cheaper-and-lighter computing front included Apple's pocket-sized Newton, an executive organizer with built-in wireless communications, and notebooks with an

Hubble Telescope

electronic pen replacing the keyboard. For the most part, the pen systems ultimately flopped.

Silicon Graphics acquired MIPS Computers in 1992 when a financial crisis beset that company. MIPS continued to operate as a unit of Silicon Graphics, building the powerful computers that run its 3-D graphics. The two companies had collaborated closely in past years.

Compression Labs, Inc. (CLI), market leader in videoconferencing technologies and systems, in 1992 introduced the VideoPhone 2500, which CLI worked with AT&T to develop. Compression technology was opening the way for display of video clips on computers and other advances. Multimedia—shorthand for the addition of fine audio and video capabilities to standard computer attributes—was on the way to becoming a standard feature of "loaded" PCs.

At last responding to the demands of consumers and corporate data processing managers, a computer industry consortium formed, promising to make all workstation computers run the same open operating system, thereby freeing customers to buy any supplier's software. However, "middleman" programs designed to run between the software and the operating system emerged, relieving some of the open-systems pressure.

The U.S. government began a move to create nationwide "superhighways for data," an outgrowth of legislation proposed by Senator Al Gore Jr. to speed up an existing network. High speeds were needed to link supercomputers and, via the Internet, make their power available to smaller universities, libraries, and government research centers.

New on the semiconductor front were 8-inch silicon wafers, produced in an Intel fab in Santa Clara. New advances in manufacturing technology had enabled this step toward increased efficiency. In 1991, meanwhile, Intel had ceased further development of the EPROM in favor of flash memory development. Flash memory chips retain data even when computer system power is turned off.

Richard Robert Ernst won the 1991 Nobel Prize for chemistry for broadening the usefulness of high-resolution nuclear magnetic resonance (NMR) spectroscopy. Ernst, a Swiss professor, had spent five years as a research scientist at Varian Associates in Palo Alto where, with U.S. colleague Weston A. Anderson, he made one of the discoveries cited for his award. His work built upon earlier studies by Stanford's Felix Bloch, a 1952 Nobelist. Until Ernst's refinements, NMR had been a tool for chemistry; after his refinements, it served also in physics, biology, and medicine.

Biotechnology firms, once clustered mainly near San Francisco and Berkeley, had spread in large numbers to central Silicon Valley. Venture capital firms were investing heavily in them.

Silicon wafer

1991

Gorbachev resigns, saying Soviet Union no longer exists.

1992

Treaty signing ends El Salvador's 12-year civil war.

U.S. President George Bush and Russian President Boris Yeltsin declare end of Cold War.

North and South Korea sign pacts aimed at reunification.

China tests large nuclear device.

Panamanian strongman Noriega sentenced to 40 years in prison.

Atrocities prompt UN to declare Yugoslavia's seat vacant.

1993

Czechoslovakia splits into Czech Republic and Slovakia.

Rival military factions sign Afghanistan peace plan.

Waco standoff ends in tragedy.

Danish voters narrowly approve union with Europe.

The body of former President Marcos is returned to Philippine Republic for burial.

Sihanouk becomes Cambodian king for second time.

The Vatican and Israel reach an accord.

South African Communist Christopher Hani is assassinated.

Melchior Ndadaye, president of Burundi, is assassinated.

Chapter 17: Surfing on the Internet

The Internet caught the public's fancy in 1993-94. Originally noncommercial in nature and without much funding or central management, it was simply a linkup of diverse computer networks based at academic or research centers. Then software companies introduced products to make the Internet easier to use, on-line services opened gateways into it, and personal computer users became able to sign on.

As people began to grasp the Internet's possibilities—spurred by a Washington champion, Vice President Al Gore—the user count expanded phenomenally. Intrigued by all the activities they could carry on in cyberspace, computer buffs spent hours exploring the Net just for fun.

Ed McCracken of Silicon Graphics voiced the wonder of it: "We are experiencing the information revolution—the ability to communicate with anyone, anytime, and anywhere."

Although companies in many parts of North America, Europe, and Asia were racing to capitalize on the Internet, a good deal of the activity was concentrated in Silicon Valley in companies large and small. Installations of fiberoptic cables, high-speed switches, and wireless transmitters were in progress around the San Francisco Bay, and Cupertino and Palo Alto were among the cities gaining an early place on the Net. Smart Valley, a Palo Alto-based nonprofit consortium, aimed to spur development of a regional infrastructure in order to revitalize education, reduce health care costs, create jobs, and make local government more responsive.

In 1993, ultrasmall computing systems equipped with wireless networking systems came into vogue. Both they and home and office computers were offered the promise of networking with other computers on a data superhighway.

At the movies, meanwhile, fans' eyes were popping. Silicon Graphics' 3-D imaging was behind many of the extraordinary technical effects that seemed to bring prehistoric animals to life in Steven Spielberg's 1993 movie, *Jurassic Park,* a box office record-setter. Then came *Forrest Gump,* with scenes of its slow-witted hero in action with dead Presidents John F. Kennedy and Lyndon B. Johnson.

The same year saw the debut of a new product promoting connections between PC users: PCMCIA cards. Named for its designer, the Personal Computer Memory Card Industry Association, the device, about the size of a business card, but thicker, could be inserted in a slot in a pocket-size computer to give it special functions such as extra memory. Later, the name was simplified to PC cards.

Handheld personal digital assistants—PDAs—also bowed in. The palm-size computers had no keyboards; instead, users wrote on a plastic grid with a special pen. There was no standard operating system, and a consortium called General Magic formed to try to develop the proper software.

Two computer giants' marketplace skids led to ousters of John Sculley at Apple Computer and John Akers at IBM. Borland International of Scotts Valley, once seen as a major PC software player, entered deep decline.

A new Cray Y-MP C90 supercomputer—the world's fastest—was added to Ames Research Center's NAS program equipment. It upped Ames's computing power more than sixfold. The C90 can do more than 6 billion calculations per second, and can hold 1 billion words in memory.

Space shuttle Endeavour's crew successfully repaired the Hubble Space Telescope in orbit. Many rated the fix-it mission NASA's biggest test since the 1969 moon landings.

On July 1, 1994, the Navy disestablished Moffett Field Naval Air Station, and NASA's Ames Research Center began managing the facility as Moffett Federal Base. Since 1987, Ames had operated its 14th wind tunnel—the largest wind tunnel on earth for aerodynamic testing.

Computer and telecommunications firms were converging, as evidenced by AT&T bidding to merge with McCaw Cellular, the largest U.S. independent cellular company, and Bell Atlantic seeking to buy cable television conglomerate TCI, Inc., so as to use TCI lines outside its own service area to carry telephone calls. (The Bell Atlantic-TCI deal later fell through.) Cable TV companies could compete with telephone companies, which in turn wanted to enter the cable TV business to finance laying of fiberoptic cable to homes.

Intel Corp. in 1993 unveiled its fifth-generation microprocessor, the Pentium, packing 3.1 million transistors and capable of executing more than 1 million instructions per second (MIPS). Motorola brought out a rival chip family, the PowerPC microprocessors, developed jointly in conjunction with IBM Corp. and Apple Computer.

Late in '94, the Internet became the medium carrying harsh consumer criticism of Intel for its reluctance to replace Pentiums after a flaw affecting complicated division problems was revealed. At length the company bowed to public opinion and offered a replacement to any owner who asked for it, at a cost estimated at $475 million.

In early 1995 Intel and Advanced Micro Devices settled their legal battle, begun in 1987 after Intel declined to share its 386 microprocessor technology with AMD, which then cloned the chip. During the litigation, Intel had brought out its i486 and the Pentium; AMD had brought out a 486 and was at work on K-5, a fifth-generation microprocessor of its own design.

1994

Disastrous earthquake devastates Los Angeles suburbs.

Israel and the PLO begin to grant Gaza and West Bank self-government.

European Union welcomes Austria, Finland, and Sweden.

World trade pact is finally signed.

Nelson Mandela becomes South African president after first multiracial voting.

Channel Tunnel linking France and Britain inaugurated.

Hubble Telescope proves Einstein's "black hole" theory.

International terrorist "Carlos the Jackal" nabbed in Sudan.

Impasse halts U.S. health care debate.

1995

GOP takes control of Congress, led by Bob Dole, Newt Gingrich.

Oklahoma City courthouse bomb kills 168.

Census Bureau says Americans are staying put more nowadays.

Chicago heat wave kills 450.

Women meet, assert rights in Beijing, China.

Affirmative action ended by UC Regents.

Belarus shoots down 2 U.S. balloonists.

U.S. reopens diplomacy with Hanoi.

Jury acquits O.J. Simpson of murders.

U.S. stocks soar; Dow breaks 5,000.

Princess Di tells troubles on television.

Mexican peso skids against U.S. dollar.

Budget tussle shuts down government.

Chapter 18: A Vintage Year in Silicon Valley

For most of Silicon Valley, 1995 was a vintage year, perhaps the best ever. Booming sales of computers, chips, and semiconductor equipment sent technology stocks surging in the first half of the year. By the three-quarters mark, the science and technology mutual funds index was up 46.7%, and a number of the larger companies had registered market-value increases of near 100% — some 200% or more. Barring anything like the October 1987 crash, 1995 promised to end with many record gains.

Amazingly fast growth occurred in much of Silicon Valley industry. Demand ran high for computers and peripherals, semiconductors, semiconductor manufacturing equipment, communications devices, and multimedia products. Biotechnology did not generally share in the boom. Venture capital firms were active. Companies bought land, erected buildings and hired again after a long no-growth period. Seeking to cash in on the Internet's popularity, online, database, computer, networking, telephone, and cable television companies were all scrambling for position.

Technology advanced rapidly, too, spurring intense competition in some arenas. In disk drives, for example, new product generations lasted only nine months, prices fell 12% each quarter, and companies had to increase the storage capacity on a disk 60% a year to keep pace with their rivals. Large hard disks commonly stored 1.6 gigabytes, more than 50 times as much data as a decade earlier.

This pace forced one major consolidation. Seagate Technology Inc. agreed to acquire Conner Peripherals. The purchase of the No. 3 disk-drive company by the No. 2 company would create one company with $7.5 billion in revenues.

Early in 1995, Intel and Advanced Micro Devices settled their long legal battle, begun in 1987 after Intel declined to share its 386 microprocessor technology with AMD, which then cloned the chip. During the litigation, Intel had brought out its i486 and the Pentium; AMD had brought out a 486 and was at work on K-5, a fifth-generation microprocessor of its own design.

The hottest initial public offering turned out to be Netscape Communications Corp., a Mountain View firm founded by James H. Clark, who earlier founded Silicon Graphics, Inc. The stock more than tripled before settling back a bit, but wild action on the initial public offering signaled keen interest in simple ways to access — and do business on — the Internet.

Image captured by Hubble Space Telescope shows details of formation of new stars

In computer networking, acquisitions and mergers were rife. Three growing companies, each already well past $1 billion in revenues, appeared locked in a battle for dominance. Out in front were Cisco Systems of San Jose and 3Com of Santa Clara, which made its 11th acquisition in four years (not counting putting its name on the San Francisco stadium formerly known as Candlestick Park). Also in the derby was Bay Networks, formed of a recent merger of SynOptics of Santa Clara and Wellfleet of Massachusetts.

In software, introduction of Microsoft's Windows 95 operating system took the spotlight in August. But before that, Microsoft — under pressure from the Justice Department — dropped its bid to make a $2 billion purchase of Intuit Inc., the maker of the popular Quicken and TurboTax personal finance programs. Intuit employees in Menlo Park reportedly cheered when the deal collapsed. Oracle Corporation, Silicon Valley's largest software company, had its eye on the Internet, and so did Adobe Systems.

In microprocessors, Intel pressed its hot-selling Pentium advantage while rivals such as AMD, Nexgen and Cyrix aimed for faster superchips in hopes of reducing Intel's lead. Apple, IBM, and Motorola teamed up to bring out Power PC chips using RISC architecture, somewhat faster than the Pentium but possibly not enough to peel off market share.

In the workstations market, Sun Microsystems brought out the 64-bit Ultrasparc, the first major revamping of its Sparc architecture since 1987, claiming unique multimedia features. Hewlett-Packard, Digital Equipment Company, and Intel with its projected P6 were working on faster-rated workstation chips for future introduction. MIPS Technologies, a Silicon Graphics subsidiary, had fielded its R10000 processor, "the fastest yet." Pyramid Technology was grouping MIPS and other chips in what Pyramid called "the most robust massively parallel offering."

Imagine testing a nuclear weapon with a computer. The U.S. Department of Energy announced a contract for Intel to develop a supercomputer using 9,000 P6 processors that would be capable of simulating nuclear weapons tests — without the fallout.

In the shrinking U.S. defense industry, Lockheed and Martin Marietta completed their $10 billion merger as Lockheed Martin Corp. When worker layoff plans were announced, Lockheed Missiles and Space Company in Sunnyvale — already down from a peak of nearly 25,000 employees to 11,000 — escaped major cuts, indicating its projects would continue little changed in the near term. At adjoining Moffett Federal Base, a struggle was on to repel proposals to reduce Ames Research Center's role within NASA.

Driven by the desire to avoid a rerun of the VHS-Beta war of decades past, global companies planning to manufacture digital video disks compromised on a single standard. A group of seven manufacturers led by Toshiba Corp. accepted a proposal from the other camp, led by Philips Electronics and Sony Corp. Alan Bell, a specialist in CD technology at IBM's Almaden Research Center in San Jose, headed a computer industry workgroup, including representatives of Apple, HP, Sun, and other companies, that successfully urged a single CD technology that would meet their needs.

The new disk will store a 133-minute movie at the highest audio and video quality, or store audio and computer data and software. It will have more than seven times a CD-ROM's computer data capacity. *The New York Times* said the process behind the agreement reflected the convergence of the consumer electronics, computer, and entertainment industries as a single multimedia industry.

Another ballyhooed form of convergence, that of computers and telecommunications, was cast into doubt when AT&T abandoned its costly vision of operating as a single corporate empire and divided itself into three companies.

Pixar IPO nets Steve Jobs a paper billion.

Gov. Pete Wilson quits as candidate for president.

Israeli president Itzhak Rabin assassinated.

Gen. Colin Powell won't run for office.

Japan makes apology to World War II 'comfort women.'

Papers run Unabomber's manifesto.

Fans mourn slain pop singer Selena.

New Zealand yacht wins America's Cup.

Clinton OKs closing of 105 military bases.

Protests greet French A-tests in Polynesia.

U.S.-Russian space linkup first in 20 years.

Kiss-stealing senator resigns rather than face accusers.

Chapter 19: Peering into the Future

How far into the future can the Silicon Valley Renaissance carry? Until 2000 A.D.? For another generation or two? Another century? For 500 years?

Five to ten years ago there was talk of the greying of the Valley, of its becoming "another Detroit," of Japan Inc. having stolen its magic while taking over the chips production lead.

Today Silicon Valley again is sitting on top of the world in its chosen fields: semiconductor production, microprocessor power, semiconductor equipment manufacture, storage systems, 3-D and other specialized chips, lasers, logic devices, personal computers, networking equipment, and a clutch of other fields. Japan is second in chips, with its Asian rivals challenging. At Hewlett-Packard, the Valley's most mature big company, the success of new top management has quelled all talk of "greying." Certain other companies are profiting handsomely from mature managers' strategies. In the midst of a banner year, worries about the capability of upcoming technical and management talent rarely are heard.

Certainly, things change fast in high technology, but the likelihood of Silicon Valley's applecart being upset before the advent of the 21st century is minuscule. During the 20th century, the United States has led the world in the successful application of inventions, and in the past two decades Silicon Valley has clearly led the United States.

As the new century approaches, Silicon Valley has a tremendous "installed base" — arguably the world's greatest high-tech aggregation of creative companies, rich in brainpower, financial power, research power, and know-how. Supporting them is a peerless infrastructure of venture capitalists, specialized law and accounting firms, management consultants, marketing experts, suppliers, and specialty service providers.

In the near term, many technological advances are already scheduled. Target dates for two new generations of microprocessors have been announced by companies in that race, and the front-runners are momentarily in sync with the calendar: sixth generation in 1996, seventh in 1997. Although theorists worry that physics may impose limits on further miniaturization of transistors and circuits, leading-edge production is well into the sub 0.5-micron range and no evidence of "hitting the wall" has caused alarm. More powerful network servers are in the offing. In the multimedia field, new chips are blooming in profusion. Silicon Valley companies are in the thick of the effort to improve Internet access, enhance wireless communications, and many another technological advance.

Business strategies, too, portend keen competition just ahead. Scott McNealy of Sun Microsystems, the largest seller of workstations, recently spoke of branching out to the consumer market through its Sparc chip in next version of Netscape and through a personal computer device—"a little flat-panel notebook thing with a fast microprocessor." McNealy was openly scornful of Microsoft's Windows 95. Intel's efforts to make its microprocessors serve more functions are taken as a threat by some makers of specialty chip sets. Mergers and acquisitions surely will continue, and now and then a competitor will collapse.

The battle by personal computer, telecommunications, and cable television companies for shares of each other's turf will soon be fully joined. Globe-girdling satellite systems, some of them built in the Valley, and fiber optic networks are deeply involved in this face-down.

Somewhat further off are the fruitions of new technologies that might challenge today's established kingpins: DNA computing, nanotechnology or molecular engineering, optical storage employing holograms, neural networks, superconductors, and "smart" system applications, to name a few. Despite the giant strides of "going digital" in the last few years, analog or linear devices also are scoring new breakthroughs.

In biotechnology, the Human Genome Project, a U.S.-led effort to decipher the entire human genetic code, is projected for completion by the year 2005. The promise of a vast future in genetic engineering has attracted strong venture capital support.

Not everything about the future is bright. The unabated global increase in human population is probably the greatest threat to the future. Severe over-population problems continue to affect the environment, economics and prospects for world peace. Anti-technology attitudes are marked in the so-called Generation X, although it is also manifest that capable young scientists are coming from the under-30 age group. As reliance on the Internet increases, both domestically and in international communication, the risk of catastrophic breakdowns grows. In his recent book, *Computer-Related Risks,* Peter G. Neumann, principal scientist in SRI International's computer science laboratory, warns that "serious disasters" lie ahead. Neumann calls for a global perspective in determining which are the real risks and which techniques can have the most significant payoffs over time. His analysis is based on familiarity with past problems—usually human shortcomings that are passed off as "computer glitches."

Many leading Silicon Valley figures expect the surge of the 1990s to go on for a quarter century, at least. A number of them say we have seen only the beginning.

Those who are tempted to think that opportunity has been exhausted in the 20th century might harken to David Packard, who pointed out in his book, *The HP Way,* that most of the progress of those 100 years or so stemmed from scientific discoveries made by the end of the 19th century. Since then, high-energy physics research (at SLAC and elsewhere) has discovered that the atom itself contains smaller particles that do not obey the Newtonian laws of physics, he wrote, adding:

"... with the new understanding of the atom, we can create materials that do not occur in nature ...offering a whole new world of scientific opportunity. Everywhere I look I see the potential for growth, for discovery far greater than anything we have seen in the 20th century."

Speaking to HP employees in Switzerland late in 1994, Packard remarked: "So you young people have wonderful futures to look forward to and it's going to be an exciting world for you."

Dave Packard, founder
Hewlett - Packard Company

INDEX

—T—

—U—

—V—

—W—

—X—

—Y—

—Z—